In The Shadow Of His Wings

By Barbara Thomson

McKnight & Bishop Ltd

CW01597602

About the Publisher

McKnight & Bishop are always on the look-out for new authors and ideas for new books. If you write or if you have an idea for a book, please e-mail us at:
info@mcknightbishop.com

Some things we love are undiscovered authors, open-source software, Creative Commons, crowd-funding, Amazon/Kindle, social networking, faith, laughter and new ideas.

Visit us at www.mcknightbishop.com

Scripture quotations taken from the Amplified® Bible (AMPC), Copyright © 1954, 1958, 1962, 1964, 1965, 1987 by The Lockman Foundation. Used by permission. www.Lockman.org

Cover image rights: Wings – Freepik.com | Clouds – onlyyouqj

Copyright © 1991 by Barbara Thomson

The right of Barbara Thomson to be identified as the Author of the Work has been asserted by her in accordance with the Copyright, Designs and Patents Act 1988.

All rights reserved. No part of this publication may be reproduced, stored in a retrieval system, or transmitted, in any form or by any means without the prior written permission of the publisher, nor be otherwise circulated in any form of binding or cover other than that in which it is published and without a similar condition being imposed on the subsequent purchaser.

The views expressed in this work are solely those of the author and do not necessarily reflect the views of the publisher, and the publisher hereby disclaims any responsibility for them.

ISBN 978-1-905691-60-9
A CIP catalogue record for this book is available from the British Library
First published in 2019 by McKnight & Bishop Inspire, an imprint of:

McKnight & Bishop Ltd. | 26 Walworth Crescent, Darlington, DL3 0TX
http://www.mcknightbishop.com | info@mcknightbishop.com

This book has been typeset in Arial, Garamond-Normal, Lovely Home, Brush Script MT and Rockwell

Printed and bound in Great Britain by Cloc Ltd

Introduction

> "Love the Lord your God with all your heart and with all your soul and with all your mind and with all your strength."
>
> Mark Ch 12 v 30

In mid 1977 these scriptures stood out at me as I was attending Mass. They were printed in the form of a prayer following communion. I must have seen them countless times before but that time they were speaking to me and my response could only be I don't know you and I can't see you. How can I love you like that?"

My second baby, Neil, was in my arms. I had lost my first baby, Paula, tragically in October 1975. Neil's birth had brought such joy. I could see him, know him and love him so much. My husband, John, was at home. He did not attend church with me but always encouraged me to go. I thought of him and knew how much I loved him and that if these words in front of me were really true, I obviously did not know this God to love him at all.

Attending church and living with regulations had not caused me to know this God enough to love him or see him in any real way. So my desire "To know him" began. Now as I write, these scriptures stand out again, strong and clear. My Pastor preached on them just two weeks ago, just as I was preparing my thoughts about a Celebration and Thanksgiving Service to God for sparing my life to serve him.

I have been on a journey for 14 years, through joy and pain, and I want to tell you of the journey and my desire "TO KNOW HIM." Paul expresses it so well in his letter to the Philippian Church as recorded in Chapter 3 and verses 10 -14 when he tells of his own personal purpose in life to know The Lord Jesus Christ. The joy of knowing Him and yet knowing there is more. The joy of loving Him, knowing that He loves me more. This enables me to serve him more and gives me the great desire to be obedient to him and to write this book in His name.

Chapter 1

> "Here I am. I stand at the door and knock. If anyone hears my voice and opens the door, I will come in and eat with him, and he with me."
>
> Revelation Ch 3 v 20

I had always attended Mass as part of my life having been brought up as a Roman Catholic. Sometimes it felt good just to belong. I was comfortable in the ritual. I enjoyed meeting with friendly faces. At times I didn't feel like going but I was under an obligation. However since the scripture in Mark Ch 12 v 30 "Love The Lord your God with all your heart and with all your soul and with all your mind and with all your strength" had spoken to me, I loved to go and listen to the priest preaching. He was a man who obviously knew God personally.

I listened to him and seemed drawn somehow. Words would stick out about knowing this JESUS in a way I had not understood before. I always knew that Jesus was God's son who died on the cross for "US", who rose on the third day and was now in heaven. We had songs to him and talked about his teachings. My understanding of God was that of one who was sitting in judgment over me. I always hoped that the day I died I would have just been to confession so that I would have no sin on me, so allowing me into heaven, but knowing how easily I could fall into sin.....THEN WHERE WOULD I GO? I imagined a great big set of scales with my sin on one side and my good deeds and penances on the other.

The fact that JESUS died for "ME" and paid the price for all my sin had not been something that I had understood. As I listened to this priest he talked about a personal love and "an openness of heart" to God. This second point puzzled yet fascinated me. The priest encouraged the congregation to read the Bible, so I bought one and had it blessed. I felt so pleased with myself, thinking that this would add a bit of weight to my good deeds. I started to read the bible from the beginning. That feeling of pride in myself soon left me as I read about so many "Begats" that I felt it "Begot me nowhere". I did not know why I could not get into it or understand it.

At the same time I grew in desire to help others. I had trained and registered as a General Nurse and also as a Mental Nurse. This gave me the confidence to talk about medical and mental health problems and so I joined a voluntary organisation who visited people within the parish to fulfil this desire. Again pride in my own works caused me to think that this would please this God who sits in judgment of me. I was proving that I was trying to love him.

At the same time, my sister Margaret, who lives in New Zealand, had realised that there was more to life than how she was living. These thoughts had caused her to search for a deeper meaning and purpose for her life. She did not seem to be getting any answers and this had depressed her, so when we visited her in December 1977 she envied my newly found true desire to go to church and listen to the preacher. For the seven weeks that we were with her she came to church with me, wanting to experience the same joy, but it did not work for her.

However, when I had returned home, she wrote to tell me that she had had a total stranger call at her door. He was a "Born-again Christian." Neither of us had heard of the term before. I thought that all Protestants were all the same. He had been an answer to Margaret's cry from her heart, her own desire to know God. He had caught her attention with the words "DO YOU REALLY KNOW THE LORD?" Because of my own experience, these words touched me too. After some time, and a few more visits from this man, Margaret committed herself to Jesus. She called it "I HAVE GIVEN MY HEART TO THE LORD." These words were strange to my ears yet somehow connected to what my priest was saying. It was the same theme that was drawing me.

As 1978 progressed, letters from New Zealand were laced with phrases 'PRAISE THE LORD' and 'HALLELUJAH.' I thought, "She's gone totally over the top. She jumps on any bandwagon." I wanted her to go to church but this was just too much for my understanding of "everything done in order." I did not expect it to last but her letters kept coming in the same vein. There was something about these letters, and as I read between the lines, I sensed a joy and a personal knowledge of God that I longed for myself.

Now pregnant with my third child, I was anxious and upset. Having lost one baby, I knew how easily it could happen again. Paula, my first child, had been born with a hole in her heart. She had lived only 15 days. Neil's birth had brought with it much healing from the grief but it was to be much later before I was free from the guilt. I had shared my fears and anxiety with Margaret. Her reply was, "PRAY AND JUST TRUST JESUS." This made me angry. I had not blamed God for Paula's death but even in my limited understanding of God, I knew that He knew that I had prayed every night for her to be born well. Margaret's somewhat glib statement fell to the ground. I wondered how she would feel if it happened to her. It was only much later that I was to realise that my lack of a personal relationship with God led to a lack of trust in him.

Baby number three, Philip, was born. It was the easiest of deliveries. He was perfect in every way and very much a blessing to all of the family.

Seven months later (July 1979) Margaret came to visit us with her husband and son. She was to split her time in this country between us and her husband's relatives. When we met, I immediately saw in her something new, but I couldn't put my finger on it. Two years had passed since since I first desired to know the Lord. In the meantime I had moved house into another parish. The preaching still stimulated my desire to know The Lord, but the priest was not as charismatic. On reflection, perhaps he did not have the same personal relationship with God as the previous priest had.

Margaret's first visit was short. She had a lot to do, but she left a book for me to read: *The Seal of God* by F.C.Payne (revised and reprinted by E.R.Finck). She had been praying for me with her friends for months, and she expected to see a move of

God in my life. As I read the book that feeling of adding to the good side of the scales was with me, especially when my neighbour looked over the garden fence. I was proud to tell her that I was reading all about God. She was not interested after that and went back indoors. What was amazing was that I couldn't stop reading it. I was intrigued at how it talked about the bible being given to us by the inspiring work of The Holy Spirit. As it went on to talk about numbers and symbols in Hebrews, it proved to me without a shadow of doubt, that no human being could have been so clever to write the bible on his own. That indeed, I believed, by the Holy Spirit writing through man, God's purposes plans and miraculous interventions at times, are recorded, and are alive to us today by that same spirit. That was something new for me to think about. It made me say “WOW”. I had previously thought it was just a load of stories. There it was. That same God who inspired the bible was speaking to me personally through Revelation Ch 3 v 20.

“Here I am. I stand at the door and knock. If anyone hears my voice and opens the door, I will come in and eat with him, and he with me”

There I was in my own living room. My husband and children were in bed. I responded. I took my right hand and opened an imaginary door in my chest. I invited the Lord Jesus Christ in as Lord over my life. I asked him to shut the door after him and never to leave again. HE HASN'T. Words would fail to explain the experience that followed. An overpowering presence, something that the best warm glow of receiving love from an individual could not match. I was tingling from head to foot. A real feeling. A joyous feeling. I had set off to know him. It appeared that I had met him in a way that he had been waiting for me to respond in. I had not imagined it. No one had told me that this would happen. It was real and could not be explained away to rob me of it. I believed My Lord had indeed come in to eat with me.

Chapter 2

> Jesus replied "Let it be so now it is proper for us to do this to fulfil all righteousness."
>
> Matthew Ch 3 v 15

How could anyone understand me? I had gone to church all of my life. Why was I now behaving as if all my experiences were brand new? That is how it felt. I was reading the bible with such joy. My eyes seemed to have been opened to see what once I could not see in those beautiful words, speaking to me so clearly and making me want more. I told everyone who was prepared to listen about my new experience. I had been 'BORN AGAIN.' The experience explained the words. Jesus was my Lord. He could have his way in my life and communicate with me about that will through the inspired word of God – THE BIBLE.

Margaret visited our home again. She felt that she could not speak freely to me about spiritual matters because our husbands were around and they did not understand our interest in such things. As she was leaving she asked me whether I had read the book and if I had done anything about it. I replied positively to both questions and added that I had asked The Lord Jesus to live in my life now and forever. I saw her literally skip down our driveway with joy. It took me by surprise but I was later to feel that joy she was experiencing as The Lord allowed me to witness someone stepping from the kingdom of darkness into the Kingdom of the Son He loves (Colossians Ch 1 v 13) but at that point I found it a little unexpected and indeed, embarrassing.

We had a fortnight camping holiday in Wales with Margaret, her husband and son. Margaret and I were able to spend some time together, talking and praying. This was the sum total of my nurture course as a new Christian. She gave me another book called "Nine o'clock in the morning" by Dennis Bennett which talked about the practical experiences of the use of The Gifts of The Holy Spirit as the bible records in 1 Corinthians Ch 12-14. I had never received any teaching on this subject before but there was something within me that caused me to know that this was right and true. It gave me the desire to be filled with The Holy Spirit and to have these miraculous gifts work through me. The term used was "Baptism in the Holy Spirit."

Listening to Margaret using the gift of tongues was just amazing to me. I wanted it. I knew that it was something miraculous but if Margaret could have it, then so could I. Margaret prayed for me to receive The Holy Spirit and laid her hands upon me as described in Acts Ch 8 v 17. I expected to speak with the gift of tongues but nothing happened. Disappointed, I settled for the recent Born Again experience and the joy of reading the bible, praying more openly and telling others about this.

I still wanted the gifts of the Holy Spirit to be working through me. My sister spoke in faith over me (another gift of the Holy Spirit) before she left the country and told me that I would be speaking the new language within weeks, and indeed I was.

It was first brought to my understanding that it is The Person of the Holy Spirit that we seek. Jesus spoke about asking The Father to give us The Person of The Holy Spirit in John Ch 14 v 16. We first accept this, give ourselves over to God's purposes. We give our tongue to him, believing that we will be given a new language to praise him and communicate with him by our own spirit.

I sat one night in prayer before The Lord and began repeating the word “Abba, Abba,” to The Lord, believing that I would indeed speak in the Spirit Language. “Abba” is an Aramaic word for “Father,” but only used in a private and intimate way, never in public by a Jewish child. A translation would be “Daddy” (Romans Ch 8 v 15). As a new baby gives out syllables before proper words are formed, in the same way I was using my own tongue for the Holy Spirit to form words, believing in faith that this would happen. Suddenly my tongue started to trip up and then freely took off, sounding like an American Indian. What a thrill!

I remembered back to a few nights earlier when I had dreamed that I was actually speaking in Tongues with my arms in the air waving about. I did not know that this would become a natural thing to do as I praised the Lord in the spirit. I had not seen anyone else do this. God had shown me yet again how these were of him and not just me imitating someone else. I praised him for the specific way in which he confirmed this teaching to me.

My new life in Jesus Christ was not all joy. The church that I was attending was run by a priest who found my questioning a burden as I searched for the truth. I would read the bible and then see or hear something at church that seemed to conflict, so I would question him. As we talked together he would understand where I had got my information from and agree with the point that I was making. He would explain that others did not understand as I was understanding, and that the things I questioned actually helped them.

An example was the Confessional Box. He told me that it was all right for me to think in the way that I did as long as I did not express myself publicly. This confused and troubled me. I longed for some like-minded people to share with me and perhaps understand my thirst for the truth. I prayed to this end.

By chance (or was it a Divine Appointment?) I met someone at a neighbour's house. She mentioned a midweek meeting that took place at the Hospital Chapel. She described it as the meeting of The Hallelujah Chorus. I felt that she wanted me to join with her in criticising these strange meetings, but in my spirit, I felt that it could be an answer to prayer for me.

I went along and found that it was led by a Born again, Spirit filled, Roman Catholic Priest from another parish in Darlington. It was in fact an inter-denominational meeting known as the Charismatic Renewal Meeting. I began to attend regularly and with this, together with inspired teaching on tapes by Margaret from New Zealand, I grew slowly but surely.

This satisfied me for a while until more questions about the teachings of the Catholic Church arose. Some of these questions were answered unknowingly by the priest who led the midweek meeting. He caused me to see that we serve The Lord and therefore the Church and not the other way around. Now The Lord is a personal Lord and I had truly experienced this, and he brings peace. I knew that he could show me the way to serve him. The priest had stated that he himself had stayed within the Catholic Church and obeyed its teachings because The Lord had told him personally to do so. It made me think that if The Lord had told him to move, he would have done so.

It made me ask The Lord what he wanted of me personally. There was a growing desire in me to move, but a fear of offending my father. Tradition of man had a hold on me. I gave it over to The Lord. I really believed that he would clearly direct me somehow. I was willing to stay or go, as long as it was under him.

My husband, John, is a police officer. At that time he had worked in CID for a few years and was thinking about a move. To go back into uniform would mean a drop in income because of a reduction in the number of hours worked. With this in mind, we were in town one day when we passed the local Job Centre. On the "spur of the moment" I decided to have a look in to see if there were any suitable jobs for me. There was a job advertised as a Nursing Sister in a Nursing Home, 12 hours per week which I felt would cover the drop in John's income. I applied for the job, was successful and commenced work the following week. I thanked God for his provision.

As it turned out, John did not move and was in fact working even more hours. With my extra income building up in a Building Society account, I asked the Lord what it was all about. In my spirit I felt that the answer was to go to New

Zealand again to spend time with Margaret. I asked The Lord to confirm this idea. I felt that if we were to go I would be in for a real blessing. I asked him specifically to tell John to suggest the trip. I did not utter anything of my thoughts to John.

In a matter of weeks John was asking my opinion on saving up funds for another trip to New Zealand. I thanked The Lord for his confirmation, and of course I agreed with John to do this. We checked out the prices for two adults and two children with a trip to Disneyland on the way out and a stop over in Hong Kong on the way home. We looked at how much we had saved since I started working and calculated that it would take about two years to save the required funds.

I wrote to Margaret about our desire to visit. She was pleased and joined with my prayers. She too heard from The Lord and confirmed to me that it would indeed be a time of special blessing. It seemed ironic, but with a couple of serious incidents occurring in the town, plus a rise in income for John, we actually had the fare saved in six months. God was truly in charge and we set off in February 1981 for a six week holiday.

It was good to be with Margaret. I felt very welcomed by her Christian friends and joined in with their Bible Study Group. I shared with them that I knew that I was due to receive a very specific blessing but at that time I was unsure what it was. Margaret asked me if I had thought about the need to be baptised in water. I immediately answered that I did not need to. She did not push the point but left it with me.. The leader of the study group asked me to prepare a study. The title was of all things "Water Baptism." I felt privileged and encouraged to have been asked, and used Margaret's Concordance to collect the material. All that was expected of me was to present the material at the meeting for discussion.

Whilst I was preparing these scriptures in Margaret's house, she mentioned again that maybe I DID need to be baptised. At that point, I lost my temper with her, walked into my bedroom and slammed the door. My bible was open on my bed where I had left it. I cried out to The Lord "What do you think Lord? I know that you can tell me."

My eyes fell onto the page of the open bible. Matthew Ch 3 v 15 stood out at me. God was speaking to me. I could see that Jesus did not NEED to be baptised because he was without sin, but out of obedience to his father, he humbled himself and allowed John to baptise him. Verse 17 expressed that the Father (GOD) was so pleased with Jesus' obedience that he caused all those present to hear a voice telling them how much loved this son. I wanted my father God to be pleased with me. I wanted to be obedient to him no matter how I thought of my own needs. I emerged from the bedroom, bible in hand, joy within, and told Margaret of my decision. Margaret then told me that she knew that I would come through, so did her friends. I felt a little uneasy about their knowledge of me, but felt at peace with God.

I was baptised at a Baptist Church in Rotorua, New Zealand on my 30th birthday. I felt good about the future. John was in church under the power of God. He did not share my faith at all, but because it was my birthday, he could not deny me his company. God's timings are perfect. He started to speak to John that night. I answered the question about my faith in Jesus to the Minister and went under the water, dying to self and rising to The Lord. As this happened I felt that the shackles of tradition had fallen off, and that I could now go to a church of the Lord's choosing for me.

This was that SPECIAL BLESSING.

God was directing me, knowing my need. He prepared the way.

Chapter 3

> And we know that in all things God works for the good of those who love him, who have been called according to his purpose.
>
> Romans Ch 8 v 28

My observations had shown me that man can easily, for his own purposes, interpret the Word of God wrongly. I wanted to stay open to the Holy Spirit to keep me from error. My trust had not to be in man but in God. I could trust God to work through man and I had really been encouraged by many individuals so far on my Christian walk but I had not to put them up on pedestals, expecting them to be as God. I could thank God for so many answers to prayer through individuals.

God's latest direction on my life to leave the Roman Catholic church gave me a confidence to question any teaching and expect the Bible or the work of the Holy Spirit himself to correct me and direct my steps.

Elizabeth was one of those answers to prayer for God to direct me to the place of worship where he wanted me to be. Her warmth, encouragement and genuine interest in me as I purchased books from the Elim Christian Bookshop in Darlington, where she worked, had been a stepping stone for me. The Elim Pentecostal Church in Darlington was the place the Lord wanted me to be. I am not saying that this was a perfect church or held all truth. It was the place that The Lord was directing me to and I moved in obedience.

I arrived nervously at the front gates of the church one Sunday morning to find Elizabeth about to go in. She not only took me in and introduced me to everyone, but actually took me under her wing until I felt confident in the fellowship. I was to watch her do this for many others after me. I had come home.

There was indeed a culture shock for me as we worshiped the Lord that first morning. Being so used to a formal mass, I wondered why people would stand up and seem to interrupt the proceedings from time to time. I soon got used to expecting the unexpected.

As the weeks went by it became clear to me that the Communion Table and the preaching of Jesus' death and resurrection were a very important part of the life of this church. The personal expression of members of their love for Jesus and their acceptance of his death for them as individuals in their open prayer was a special blessing for me.

My own desire to know Jesus had caused me to accept him as Lord. It was only now as his death for me, and the emphasis on the Gospel message was made more clear that I realised how much I had received when I accepted him into my life. Naively I suppose, I thought to myself if this same emphasis had been preached at my previous churches, it would not have taken me so long to come to know Jesus. There would also be a lot more Christians about who would really know HIM.

At that point everything seemed so simple. I now know there are many reasons why people can't, won't or don't believe. I remain firm though, even today, in the belief that the established church overall may lack the emphasis on the cross and the preaching of The Gospel. Traditions of Man accepts infants into the Christian Community allowing them to grow up often unchallenged by the message, “You must be born again” as described in John Ch 3 v 3.

I praise God there is a move of the Holy Spirit today to bring the revelation of the scriptures to the Body of Christ, allowing him to have his way, and so not to follow man's way or that of tradition. I think that no fellowship holds all truth, nor are they totally free from tradition. This helps me to keep humble in the knowledge that JESUS IS THE LORD OF THE CHURCH and it is HIS BODY.

Since meeting with Jesus I have dropped the denominational tag, preferring to be known as a Christian. Or a Born again Christian. I count all those who know the Lord Jesus as their Lord and Saviour as my brother or sister. Where they worship or their background does not matter. It is the relationship with Jesus that is the key. This gives me a wide view of The Church. I knew that I was called to God's purposes, and that he had directed me to Elim. I am prepared to stay or move as he directs.

Having returned from New Zealand, my wages were extra to the need for the running of the home, so again I had a chat to The Lord about it. I did not wish to become materialistic and I hated waste. In a previous prayer I had asked The Lord to prompt me on the ideal time to have another baby. As I sat before him, in my spirit, the answer was to have another baby, give up my job and I would not have to worry about the extra money. I fell pregnant that same month, rather quick for me, but it seemed to confirm God's answers to me. I looked forward to a joyous pregnancy and delivery now that I knew that Jesus was with me.

Two months into the pregnancy I had pains in my abdomen. I had a slight bleed and generally I wasn't feeling well. I had to give up my job earlier than I thought. I began to suffer the anxiety that happened with the previous pregnancies. This made me a little angry with myself. Hospital investigations showed that I was anaemic. I had been anaemic so many times before, even when I wasn't pregnant, that I was not surprised. The doctors were not too concerned about the abdominal cramps. I sat before The Lord and tried to reason with him why I could be feeling like this when I knew that the child was promised of him. The middle months of my pregnancy passed by with much less trauma. My emotions had settled, and with hindsight, I blamed my hormones for my emotional upset in the earlier months. This was probably partly true.

As I came to the sixth month I was distracted by other events surrounding my youngest sister, Christine. I feel that by outlining the background history it will enable you to understand my own involvement. I have three sisters. Margaret is 20 months my senior, Maureen is 4 years my junior and Christine who is 7 years younger than me. My brother, Peter, is the eldest in the family and 5 years my senior.

Our mother died of cancer when I was 12 years old. She had suffered a long illness before her death. Consequently Margaret and I took on the responsibility of running the home and the two younger girls looked upon us as mother figures.

Dad was at work during the day and was active in church life and the local social club on an evening. He was very supportive to us but not often at home. I think this actually helped him to overcome his own grief.

By the time I was 16, Margaret had left home and Maureen and Christine looked to me to help them. Both had attended special schools and although I did my best, with hindsight, I realised that our home life was not helpful to their emotional stability. Dad remarried when I was 18, and as I was now used to running the house in my own way, I found my own position in the house ambiguous. My step mother still had three of her eight children at home, so it was an ideal time for me to move away into Nurses Quarters at the local hospital where I was working.

I may have left home but I found that I could not lose the feeling of responsibility that I felt for Maureen and Christine. For many more years our relationship was more mother / daughter rather than that of sisters.

When Christine was 18, she suffered a psychotic nervous breakdown and was admitted as an emergency into the local psychiatric unit. By that time I had married John and because of his job, had moved from our native Hartlepool to live in Darlington. Neil was about 8 months old. At first I thought that I was ideally placed to help Christine. There had been difficulties in dad's second marriage, so it seemed a good idea for her to stay with me upon discharge from hospital, to give her space and because of my nursing background.

A weekend trial stay at my house went well, however when she came after discharge I found that caring for someone close to you for 24 hours a day was totally different from working in a hospital situation. Her delusions and sometimes hallucinations kept me awake at night. With a young child to look after as well it proved too much for me. I could not eat, I could not sleep and became tense. Dad arrived at our house following an upset at home and asked if he could stay for a while. That was the last straw. It was John that had to refuse dad's request and we took him and Christine back to Hartlepool. We felt that she required further medical attention and supervision.

I thank God that my brother Peter and his wife stepped in at that point and took both Maureen and Christine into their home until they left to marry. I had totally failed Christine and the guilt in me was horrendous. Now, as I was 6 months pregnant, Christine who was now married had given birth to a little girl and had become psychotic yet again. She had continued to look to me for advice when she was well, so her husband had contacted me thinking that I could reason with her delusions. Of course, I knew that this was not possible. I did visit her in hospital. She felt my “bump” and soon became confused about about my baby, her baby, the baby I had lost, and anybody else's baby.

In fact a lot of her delusions in previous episodes had concerned me or my family. Christine liked to see me but soon moved out of reality as we talked together. I followed her progress by contacting my father or Peter by telephone. It proved less stressful. After 6 weeks or so Christine had been allowed home with her baby, so I went to visit her. She was not as well as I had hoped from the telephone calls I had made. There seemed to be plenty of support from health care workers so I was able to encourage myself by saying it is not my problem and to walk away.

Christmas and New Year passed. My baby was due on 9th January 1982. Having had very little information from Hartlepool I took the line that no news was good news and went to visit. I found that the "no news" was a family conspiracy to keep bad news from me. Christine's baby had been injured, hospitalised and was now in care. The details were blurred. Christine was still not well. I felt good that I had been protected. I was upset with the news and I couldn't help but wonder if this was the cause of headaches that I was having. I went into hospital, my blood pressure was up and I connected this with the headaches. I put the thoughts of Christine's situation out of my mind by telling myself that I could do nothing and that I was not expected to do anything.

I settled down for the delivery. "PRAISE THE LORD" was my cry as I was delivered of another boy, Daniel. He was well, so fulfilling my preference for health over the question of sex of the child. My headache seemed worse and when checked, my blood pressure was found to be higher than when I had been admitted. I was washed, given a cup of tea, stitched and transferred to the ward. My blood pressure was checked again. By this time I was feeling quite strange – the blood pressure was continuing to rise. I was moved into a side ward and had an intravenous drip erected and drugs administered to me to bring down my blood pressure. The saying that a little knowledge is a bad thing came into play, as I realised that I could easily die, or at least have a stroke. I was 30 years old. I remembered that a man had once read my palm and told me that I would die at the age of 30 years. I longed to be 31. How was the Lord going to work this for good? I was sure that I was in his purposes. I had just given birth to this lovely baby, surely I was not going to leave him now, motherless?

Chapter 4

> You intended to harm me, but God intended it for good to accomplish what is now being done, the saving of many lives.
>
> Genesis Ch 50 v 20

My expected stay in hospital was to have been two days, but I was discharged after 9 days. It seemed even longer. A Houseman from the Psychiatric Department had paid me a visit and talked with me. He recognised that I had been ill and that it had frightened me and he prescribed a drug to help the condition that I now had: Post natal depression. This title made me angry. I did not feel depressed but I did admit to feeling like a nervous wreck, anxious about the anxiety that I felt, agitated about the agitation that I felt, and afraid of the fear that came as I would try to settle down to sleep. I felt physically unwell, dizzy and suffered palpitations. From my own training I felt that I fitted into a text book explanation of "Anxiety state" diagnosis.

I thought that I had previously understood the feelings of patients with this condition. I now knew that I was wrong.

Every time that I settled down to sleep I thought that I was going to die. No logically minded chat with myself, no prayers, nor reading of the bible could persuade me otherwise. I sometimes felt that I would not be able to take another breath, and the weight on my chest hindered the breaths that I did take.

Another problem, one that disgusted me, hit me when I least expected it. It was the fear of strangling Daniel. Just four days after his birth, I was nursing him when an uninvited thought came into my head: "If I had not had you I would not be ill now. I will kill you then I will feel better."

I shudder at this thought even now, nine years later. It repulsed me. Then a cold ugly feeling came over me, as if something was forcing me to put my hands to his throat and actually do it. I had cried out to The Lord and had held Daniel close to me until the feeling had subsided. I had to cry out to The Lord again and again until he delivered me some years later.

Daniel was a marvellous baby. I was able to breast feed him successfully which proved to be God's provision in the circumstances. The strong bond in breast feeding helped me to overcome the impulse to strangle him which came over me as if something else was doing it.

These feelings caused me to logically look at psychosis and with that came a greater fear fear of losing my own sanity. There were many members of my father's family who had suffered, and some who still were suffering with schizophrenia. John's father was a victim also. Nursing patients with this problem was one thing, but believing that I might fall victim to it, or even John himself, seemed a possibility, and the fear of it was tremendous.

My prayers, reading the bible, and the desire to know The Lord did not cease. The question, "Why?" was in every prayer. Not "Why me?" but "Why, for my own understanding, was I so ill?" Whilst I had been pregnant a visiting speaker at our fellowship informed us that he was going to call someone to the front and that they would be "Laid out in the Spirit" and from that day forth their life would be changed. He was an American and full of bounce. He called me out to the front. I was determined that I was not going to go down on the floor.

He had been telling us to bring to The Lord our most important request and believe that The Lord would answer. Also that when we knew in faith that The Lord had answered, we should speak it out as if it was already in being.

When I got to the front he asked me what I wanted most, and I replied "My husband's salvation." I did not go down in the Spirit, but the next lady to be called forward did. I did receive in faith that John would come to The Lord – and SOON.

As we sat around the lunch table that Sunday afternoon I told John about the bouncy preacher. I cannot recall John's negative reply, but I surprised myself as I told him to stop fighting faith, as he was saved already. As I spoke the words the Lord confirmed the truth of it in my spirit. I did not know how but I had received a Gift of Faith to know that John would come to The Lord.

Since having Daniel, I missed being at church. I would pray about going, speak faith over myself that I would succeed, climb into our Mini car and drive to church. I would stay two minutes then be overcome with panic attacks. I would leave and drive home very upset. John loved me so much, that even if he did not share my faith, he knew that it was upsetting me not to be able to get to church. He offered to take me, sit with me in church and hold my hand. This really was God at work. I accepted his offer and watched God reveal himself to John as he came along to meetings with me and the boys for a few months. I still panicked, but sitting at the back of the church with John, it was bearable. I really believed that The Lord put a seal on my lips as I did not question what John thought of the services.

Then one day, prompted by The Holy Spirit, I invited John to the Gospel meeting. John agreed to come and I believed that God would take care of me as it was the first time that I had been to an evening meeting since Daniel had been born.

During that week we were out as a family in the car. Daniel was now six months old. I had taken pills for four months, and in general I was no better. I believed that the pills had upset my stomach. My G.P. at that time and I did not agree so I had stopped taking the pills and decided not to see that particular doctor again.

As we were driving, I had an impulse to visit a married couple with whom I had done my psychiatric nurse training. They were both still working in psychiatry and had knowledge of the medication that I had been prescribed. I thought that I would use their knowledge to prove my thoughts correct, and have a sympathetic ear to my moans. The wife, Carol, and I had been close at one time, but I had not seen her or her husband for two years. I had shared my new faith with Carol on our last meeting and I believe that she had doubts about my sanity on that occasion.

I felt that I satisfied my query about the drug and my "Post natal depression". It seemed to me that I moaned about everything. I was still breast feeding and Daniel was due a feed. On this occasion I was not wearing a button through garment but a full dress. As I thought about it I realised that it was the first time that I had worn a dress since having Daniel. I started to make our goodbyes when Carol suggested going upstairs to feed the baby out of the way of our husbands, and four children running riot in the living room. In the quiet of the bedroom Carol actually shared a problem. I told her that if I had a problem I would pray, and I asked her if she would be able to do that. Doors of God's opportunity flew open. We made an appointment to meet the following week. Carol wanted to know this JESUS.

Until that day of our arranged meeting I had not driven out of town at all, but now I knew that with The Lord's help I could do it. I felt no panic. I arrived, we talked and prayed and I watched the Holy Spirit bring Carol into the Kingdom of God. Her husband soon followed her into faith. Exactly one week later my husband John accepted Jesus into his life. We attended Carol and her husband's baptisms. In her testimony Carol stated that I had come into her house like a breath of fresh air. I hadn't. God had by the power of his Holy Spirit and he had overshadowed us both. My illness had been used to bring at least three people into salvation. Such joy, such blessing. Praise him.

Chapter 5

> I will instruct you and teach you in the way you should go. I will counsel you and watch over you.
>
> Psalm 32 v 8

I held on to Daniel as I watched John go under the waters of Baptism. He confessed his faith in Jesus in the words from a song: "I wandered so aimless, life filled with sin, I wouldn't let my dear Saviour in, then Jesus came like a stranger in the night, Praise the Lord, I saw the light."

Tears of joy were on my face, but panic feelings were within. I thought that I would now get better. Surely God's purposes had been fulfilled in John's salvation. It was not to be. I had given myself a year to get better. We celebrated Daniel's first birthday. In all of the problems he was a real blessing. His brothers, Neil and Philip, had quite got used to helping me with Daniel as they constantly heard me saying "Mammy doesn't feel well."

As the year marker passed I sat in church on Sunday 23rd January, feeling unwell and very sorry for myself. I just cried quietly through the service repeating "WHY?"

Someone spoke in tongues.

I became so aware of the Presence of God that I knew that the interpretation of the tongue was going to speak to me. These words followed: "I know the heaviness of heart you are experiencing. It is my experience also. Have you not seen me in anguish and torment. Have you not seen my sorrow and tears. Have you not seen me bowed down because of my love and concern for those around me. Are you not yet aware of the compassion I have for those who seem helpless because of those that would come against them. Yet I have seen and understand them. I know the heaviness of your heart. I know that which would take you from my joy. But know this, that during these times of heaviness when all would be against thee, thou would learn of me. I will teach you and you will have new experiences that will be hard, but will help to strengthen others who are in anguish and torment. I love them and I am with them. So I will teach you and you will learn of me."

God had spoken to me through this Gift of the Holy Spirit in such a personal way. Just to make sure I had received it, The Lord had my friend, Ann, who was sitting next to me, confirm that the word was for me. Also, the Pastor's wife, who was sitting in front of me, turned around to tell me that all of the way through the message my name had kept going through her mind. I thanked The Lord for his confirming ways with these two witnesses. I had in fact already received it for myself and felt the Lord shake me out of my own self pity.

The words had caused me to think of Jesus hanging on the cross, bowed down for me in pain that I could never feel, desiring that all those around would know that he had gone to the cross for each one of them. He could not force people to know him or what he had done for them, yet he still took their pain and was in sorrow for their sorrow. Jesus was feeling my pain. He was with me. He was going to teach me things in his way so that I could teach others his ways. At that point it came over to me that it was alright for me to feel so much. The Lord was with me and he was going to use my experiences to help others as well as myself.

The weight that I had been feeling lifted. My attitude changed immediately as I looked with expectancy to The Lord for him to teach me. I had relied too much on my own strengths in the past. I had to rely on God's strength now and this was the first major teaching.

We are all quick to understand when Paul expresses in 2 Corinthians 12 v 9 as the Lord speaks to Paul “My power is made perfect in weakness.” It is not however so easy to grasp that “In my own strengths, I only use God in a weak way.” I desired that my strengths and weaknesses could be used for God's purposes.

Although my spirit had been lifted, I was continuing to feel physically unwell in general, and on the advice of my new lady G.P. who we met by chance outside of the supermarket (or was this another of God's ordained appointments?), I had some blood tests carried out. She had suspected Thyroid disease. The tests proved her correct and treatment with the replacement hormone Thyroxine would both correct the condition and help my general condition. It was also found that I was yet again suffering from iron deficiency anaemia. This again could be treated and I felt greatly encouraged as I knew that I would soon be feeling much better.

Thyroxine replacement did correct the thyroid disease and I could praise God for his provision. The anaemia did not respond to pills so injections and then an intravenous infusion of iron were used. Both of these caused me problems with side effects and I did not look forward to having treatment in the future. It was thought that the iron stores given to me would last for a long time without the need for further treatment. My prayers were that that I would have the ability to absorb iron from my diet correctly, as I believed that it was the lack of absorption that was causing the anaemia. This however was debatable.

My G.P. wondered whether I was losing blood from as yet unobserved areas. She talked about the use of a camera put down the food passage to check the stomach to test this theory. I refused such an examination as I could not stand the idea of a tube going down my throat whilst I was awake. Despite the general improvement in my health I still had panic attacks often linked with difficulty in breathing and swallowing. I was personally satisfied to continue to have iron replaced when needed. At that time this was acceptable to my doctor. I did have trouble with my stomach from time to time but I did not believe that bleeding from my stomach was the cause of the anaemia.

Nine months after the intravenous infusion of iron I was anaemic again. I was not prepared to receive iron other than in pill form because of my previous experiences. I believed that just because one brand of pill was unsuccessful, it did not mean that all would be the same. I did not know if my G.P.

would agree. I asked a friend to to pray that I would not have to have iron in any way other than pills.

It startled me when she said that she would pray that the fear of other treatments would be gone. Another teaching followed. I sat in prayer telling God that it was natural to be afraid of something quite different from the panic attacks, that had previously caused me problems. It was reasonable for me to ask for a miracle or for him to let the iron pills work, and that I would not accept any other answers. I suddenly visualised in my mind's eye how big God was. I felt his presence around me. In comparison I saw how tiny I was, yet here I was telling the Most High God what he had to do.

I had read the phrase from the bible "the awesome and reverential fear of God," and I think that I then understood it for the first time in reality. I did not feel condemned because of his mercy and love for me, but I started to laugh at myself. Who was I to demand that God would only work in a certain way? God has so many titles showing us who he is, his character and how he works. It was his Sovereignty that was revealed to me in that instant. I responded by saying, "I SURRENDER ALL." I also stated in faith that I wanted The Lord to freely prompt me in future if I was not surrendering to him.

God blessed me as I acknowledged him. I was able to take and absorb iron pills even if they themselves caused me some discomfort in my stomach. I was to take iron pills nearly continuously for the next three years. It was not easy to wait upon The Lord to unfold his ways of delivering me from the panic attacks. I continued to test the way forward and I now share some of his dealings with me. I got it into my head that Faith was expressed by trying to do something I was not capable of doing in the natural, and expect God to help. I continued to be disturbed from time to time with the overcoming feeling that something wanted me to kill Daniel, actually causing me to do this against my own will and desires. It did not happen at those naturally stressful times for all mothers when it is difficult to settle a crying baby. Everyone can sympathise with tension at such times. This was totally different and I wanted to help myself to overcome it. I loved babies, their smells and the "need to be needed feeling" that they gave.

My problems caused me to prefer to stand back from other babies. I decided to check out the qualifications required to be registered as a child minder. My history of Post natal depression did not hinder me, but I was asked to check with my G.P. to see if she had any reservations about my application. If she agreed then the lady at Social Services would carry out the home visit. Before going to the doctors I had prayed this prayer "I believe that within two weeks you can show me if I should go this way or not. I will not ask for the home visit until those two weeks are over."

My spirit recognised that my prayer had been heard. I made an appointment with my GP. She encouraged me to apply. PRIDE entered and as I arrived home I decided to ring Social Services and invite a home visit within the week.

As I moved towards the phone I felt a check in my spirit. "I thought you had given me two weeks to let you know if this was in me?"

The Holy Spirit was prompting me. I used to have a daily bible reading using a book "Daily Bread". I decided to check the reading for the date two weeks ahead of my original prayer.

There in bold type I read "Don't go. The Lord is not with you in this. Your enemy will overcome you."

My immediate reaction was to question whether God meant this for me in my situation. My eyes went to the bottom of the page where I read these words "The Lord means exactly what he says."

This was no coincidence. I needed to look no further for answers. Peace was within me. I was not even going to try to be a child minder.

> Let the peace of Christ [the inner calm of one who walks daily with Him] be the controlling factor in your hearts [deciding and settling questions that arise]. To this peace indeed you were called as members in one body [of believers]. And be thankful [to God always].
>
> Colossians Ch 3 v15 (AMP)

I knew that this peace had the last word. I would recognise it in many future decisions. God was dealing with me. Later I wanted to put myself in a position of trying, once again, to overcome the panic attacks. I did not see anything against going to Night School apart from feeling, in the natural, that I would not be able to succeed. Again I had not learned my lesson about being totally directed in God. I prayed for his help to let me succeed. I reasoned that this was an opportunity to meet others, learn something new, and if successful, help myself overcome fear and panic attacks.

I expected to receive more of God's help as I fasted and prayed and spoke out every positive scripture that I could think of. At that time I was learning to speak against unseen spiritual influences that from now on I will call the work of the Enemy. This includes the Devil, Satan, demons, and evil spirits. I already knew that they were around us and influenced us, causing us to fall short of God's purposes, but at that time I knew very little about the authority that I had in Christ Jesus over these things or how to use such authority by The Holy Spirit. I rebuked anything that I could think of in my prayer before I set off to night school each week. Some evenings were better than others. Occasionally I stayed the whole evening. I did enjoy all of the opportunities that it brought, but it had not helped me to overcome the panic attacks. As time went by it only added to my problem as I would feel ill for the whole day prior to night school. On the last occasion I did not even stay long enough for the class to begin. I ran out of the classroom feeling faint and dizzy. I bumped off a number of walls as I made my way along the corridors. I reached the car and drove home, crying all of the way. I hit the steering wheel in my upset and in anger. Defeated, I cried out to God "What are you doing? You have got to answer me!"

I was determined to stay up all night if necessary to receive an answer. I arrived home and waited until the family went to bed. I put my bible in front of me and sobbed. I opened the bible and without scanning the page my eyes read Ecclesiastes Ch 8 v 2-6. "Obey the King's commands I say because you took an oath before God. Do not be in a hurry to leave The King's presence. Do not stand up for a bad cause for he will do whatever he pleases. Since a King's word is supreme, who can say to him, "What are you doing?" Whoever obeys his command will come to no harm and the wise heart will know the proper time and procedure for every matter, though a man's misery weighs heavily upon him."

Again the Lord was letting me know that He had not told me to go to night school, that he truly was my Lord, and as described in Proverbs Ch 3 v 5, I should "not lean on my own understanding but in all my ways acknowledge Him and that He would make my paths straight."

It did not matter at that moment what the background was to the scripture in Ecclesiastes, or whether my use of it was in context. That was not the point. The Holy Spirit in his grace and mercy had used it to check me again. He had spoken personally into my life using words that I had even used to question God. I accepted once again that I had to wait upon God and trust him. Not just trust him to deliver me from my troubles, but to trust him because of who he is, and the fact that I had willingly given myself to him. This passage also brought over to me that God has timings for everything to be worked out. Those timings are in him, and are perfect no matter how we view them. We cannot see all that he has planned for us but we can know his love and care.

As I lay prostrate before him, I sought forgiveness for my impatience. I would not encourage anyone to make it a general rule to just open the bible and expect God to speak to you. I was desperate and God had answered me in his mercy and love. I wanted to acknowledge him, trust him and be taught by him.

Chapter 6

> I sought The Lord and he answered me. He delivered me from all my fears.
>
> Psalm Ch 34 v 4

Even though I had tried to seek ways outside of church to help myself to overcome my problems, I had not ceased to be involved in worship or work and general care towards others in the fellowship. In fact compassion had grown in my desire to help others in God's way. It was a great blessing to me to speak words of encouragement in the spirit to individuals in need. John and I had nurtured young Christians in our home and a bible study group also met weekly. I met regularly with two friends in my home as well as attending the weekly church prayer meeting. John could play a keyboard and sing, and this gave him opportunity to be used in ministry at the church. His desire to grow as a christian had led him to join the Christian Police Association. They too met at our house at times. All of these activities had a two fold purpose, a great joy fulfilled in serving The Lord, and the feeling that it helped to keep me sane. No matter how I felt before a meeting, I knew that the presence of God would settle me down as I participated.

As I looked back I could see that God was teaching me different ways of viewing my problems. My mind was taken back to the man who had read my palm and proclaimed that I would die at the age of 30. Being a teenager at the time, I had not given this any significance. Now, with hindsight, I knew that there was a real influence of evil in that incident and that until I reached the age of 31, I could not easily put it out of my mind. I had to repent of doing such things in the past as it was revealed to me that I had unwittingly allowed a curse to be put upon my life. I was pleased to get to 31 and know that the power was broken. A little more insight into these spiritual principles has shown me that the enemy could lie to me with such plausible deception about dying at the age of thirty and that I had to renounce such lies and thoughts by going back to the palm reading incident, then giving myself afresh to Jesus. This teaching opened up more revelation to renounce such things as reading Tarot cards and even reading horoscopes, not that I had done any of these things since becoming a christian, but to allow the Holy Spirit to fill all parts of me. These things may seem like fun but they are not of God and they leave us open to other spiritual influences that could have far reaching consequences in the future. No matter how trivial these things seemed to be, I knew that if my Lord was shedding his light onto these issues I must respond by walking in that light, thereby giving no legal right to the enemy to keep me in darkness.

As I have mentioned in a previous chapter, I had wondered if my experiences with the fear of harming Daniel was a symptom of psychosis. Now however, I was examining it from a different perspective. A question arose in me that challenged my own understanding yet further: "Could a Christian have the influence of a demon as described in the bible, either upon them or even in them?"

I would remind myself of the first time that I felt the impulse to strangle Daniel and the fear and the ugliness that accompanied it. I felt that it was a serious question to be explored, and I really desired an answer. It took boldness and courage to approach my pastor at that time with this question. His immediate response was that he did not know the answer but that he would get back to me. He did not get back to me and I felt quite silly about reminding him, so I left all of these thoughts open to The Lord.

I moved on, giving my time to others in need. Deep compassion motivated me to get alongside Jean. She had cancer and all the problems that go with such a devastating diagnosis. I somehow felt in a privileged position as I watched her go through fear, operation, many questions and doubts, then peace in God to meet with him. I sensed in The Lord that it was all right for Jean to prepare herself for death and heaven. She died just before Christmas 1984.

It was not all right for her husband Richard. He was one of our elders in the fellowship. I loved him as I did his wife, and I grieved with him.

I watched him overcoming the trauma of bereavement, showing Christ's character and becoming a very precious member of our fellowship.

At the same time that I had been alongside Jean, a member of John's family was terminally ill with cancer. She died a few days after Jean. Attending the two funerals, and reflecting on the deaths of both John's mother and my mother that had happened at previous Christmas times, left me with no desire to celebrate.

The following week at church, Sunday December 30th 1984, I was feeling down about the recent events and also uncomfortable with the now usual panic feelings. A message in tongues was given. I felt in my spirit that God was going to speak to me personally, and the following was given in interpretation by Bill, our other elder:

"Seek first his ways, his light, his walk. Seek these things and be in them for as you would seek these things first then others will be brought to you who need a touch of God upon their lives. That you would walk this way is the desire of God's heart for you. As you would walk this way with him he will give you the desires of your heart. For those things that seem impossible with you, all things are possible with God. For he has the ability to create all things, see he has the ability to change all situations. As you would move in faith into the things of God and give less concern to the things of your heart, and look unto him, for he is the light of all things. Look unto him concerning your situation and he will show you the way to bring you out of the situation you find yourself and bring you into light. Have no concern for yourself and your situation. Look unto him and he will reveal all truth. Things that concern you will not matter, for he will take you aside and will reveal himself unto thee, and you will walk on a new plane and the things that make you downcast will be taken away and put to one side. The ways of God are beyond your understanding.

But know this, as you would look unto him he will reveal things unto you that you have long since tackled with, and he will bring all these things to your heart and life because he loves you."

God had given me people to pray for and I was seeing results. In this message he was confirming that more people would cross my path so that he could bless them through me. I felt that the earlier promises of teaching me so that I could teach others were also being confirmed in the message, but the main thrust was that he was going to deliver me from my troubles. I was ready to go his way. I wanted his light and I was saying "Yes" to what he wanted to reveal to me. It was time, his perfect time, I believed it. I would just have to wait and see how it would come about. My spirit was lifted once again.

The following week I was having a routine blood test carried out at my doctor's surgery. My GP asked about the Christmas celebrations. I told her about the two funerals and received her sympathy. Whilst talking with her it felt right to mention my struggles with the panic attacks. I had not mentioned this problem to her for a long time and probably caused her to believe that I had recovered from them. I had not mentioned them because, basically, I did not want to take any more pills. Plus if I thought about answers, apart from the struggles I have mentioned in previous chapters, God would refer me to Psalm Ch 40 v 10: "Be still and know that I am God."

It seemed right now, and my GP advised me to see a psychologist. I came out of the surgery kicking myself for not asking if she knew of a christian psychologist, as I thought that if a stranger had to understand me, it would be easier if he shared my faith. I had visions of telling a psychologist of how

God spoke to me and being diagnosed with schizophrenia before the first session was over.

The following week in church I mentioned to Elizabeth about the need to see psychologist and my own preference for a Christian one, She told me of a man who visited the bookshop from time to time. He was a psychologist and a Christian. He worked part time for the education department and the rest of his time was freely given to God to help heal hurting Christians. This sounded good to my ears, and I took his name and telephone number from Elizabeth in order to contact him.

Even as we talked together on the telephone I knew that to see this man was the way forward for me. Gordon took a short history and encouraged me by saying that I could be helped, but that he did nothing without confirmation from The Lord. As we talked on, we both witnessed to that confirmation having been given.

He requested that an official approach be made to him through the doctor, and my doctor understood my desire to see a christian psychologist. She readily sent a letter to him.

Before the first meeting, the Holy Spirit prompted me to let his light come into every area of my life. I responded with a definite yes. When Gordon used almost the exact same words to open the counselling session I felt that God had put his seal of approval on these meetings. It emphasised that we all have a free will, and God will not work against it.

I outlined the circumstances around Daniel's birth, my sister Christine's problems and my commitment to Jesus. John was with me and Gordon talked to him about ways in which he could support me in the months ahead. I had never accepted in the past that I was suffering from a clinical depression, probably because I had seen it in others showing as a lack of care for themselves, lack of motivation, being miserable, etc, and I had none of these problems. I did accept that depression was a broad term used for problems arising after having a baby no matter how it presented itself.

Gordon caused my understanding to change and to accept that I had a clinical depression with fear syndrome. John and I were asked to make out a family tree to enable Gordon to pray over it. This was something new to me but did not cause me to challenge it in any way. My spirit was at peace as the reason for the request was explained from the scriptures. Basically, Gordon was going to pray down both of our family lines to ensure that there were no influences from the past that could affect John or the children today.

In the first meeting, Gordon finished by praying over John and me that The Lord would bring everything to memory that needed to be dealt with, and together we committed everything into The Lord's hands. I came away with a joy and expectation for the future appointments to see how God would work, knowing that I would not have received such treatment within the National Health Service.

The time between the first and second appointments was filled with problems. I really did get depressed. I felt miserable and everything that I tried to do failed. I was on the brink of being set free, yet the enemy seemed to be working overtime to keep me in fear. One night I had a nightmare. Although I had suffered many over the past three years, this one seemed worse. I awoke desiring to try and get inside of John for protection. As I clung on to him, Neil woke up vomiting. I went into his bedroom and the sight of Neil vomiting into his bedclothes made me feel like doing likewise. Usually I could cope with such sights and smells. I hurried downstairs to get a bowl and some cleaning materials. It was three o'clock in the morning. I did not see what was on the stairs but I slipped on something and down I went, flat on my back to the bottom of the stairs. I was now in shock, hurting and feeling sick. I did not know what to move first. I could hear Neil crying and I cried too.

Just for a split second my cry was "Lord why have you forsaken me?" It did not last, because even as it formed on my lips I knew that it was not true. I was literally as low as I could go and the only way that I could go was up. John had woken up with all of the commotion and he looked over the banister at me on all fours moaning at the bottom of the stairs. He had not realised that I had fallen down the stairs, but with all of the problems of late, he thought I had given up under the strain and it was time for his wife to be carted off to "The Funny Farm." Poor John. I had put him through some trial. I did appreciate him, and thanked God for him.

He wanted to get me up onto my feet still thinking I was suffering a complete nervous breakdown. I shouted in pain and let him know that I had just fallen down the stairs and that Neil needed him more than I did. As I slowly got up I started to smile to myself at the thought of how it must have given John a shock to see me crying at the bottom of the stairs at three o'clock in the morning. We told Gordon all that had happened. He did not seem surprised, the battle was at its peak.

I think it was on the third visit that Gordon prayed down the family tree with us. As he started to pray I remember thinking "Go on God, do something." At that, I felt very uncomfortable. I wanted to leave, run away as far as possible. I could hear Gordon praying. He was only praying quietly but the words that he was saying were full of power and authority. I heard him saying that he was taking authority over something. I felt more uncomfortable and could hardly keep still on the chair. Something from deep within seemed to rise up to my throat and I felt a choking sensation, then it was out. No one needed to explain what had happened, I knew that something had left me. John was moved, I was sobbing with extra large gulps. I seemed to cry from the pit of my stomach. Within my mind there had at first been a picture of my own mother, and a desire as an adult, to grieve her death.

That is what started the tears, followed by the real reason – so big and clear – fear of psychosis, not just for me but for John too. It blew up like a balloon in my mind and then left. I could say the word schizophrenia without my chest becoming tight and my stomach turning over. I knew that both sides of the family had victims to this crippling disease and I felt that I had come near to it myself, but it was only the fear of it. That is what had left me – the spirit of fear. I was free and it was so exciting. John seemed to understand too, which was a blessing to me. For the first time I was able to share my past fear of his succumbing to that disease. Only God knows why it had to be there for so long but I just thanked him for delivering me now. I really do trust his timings. He had told me to trust him and that there was a wise time for everything. I could really thank God for Gordon's obedience and ministry.

Every symptom of panic did not leave me immediately but as the weeks turned into months I could look back to that day as a turning point and view my progress. I had some unfinished business to sort out with my sister Margaret. She had not been able to understand my problems and had sent what she had thought would be helpful advice over the years. These things had just frustrated me as I realised that I wanted her understanding and her approval. I did care about what she thought about me. I wanted to discuss these things face to face. In an expression of her love towards me, Margaret had returned to work to secure funds for a visit with me. She had three children of her own now. I knew that this action had been a sacrifice for her, but she was willing to do it.

She arrived in January 1986 with her two daughters. Our time together, fellowship and prayers healed the misunderstandings and I felt that God had put a seal on my healing. I had no need to see Gordon for any more counselling. I could thank God for every trial and for the greater understanding and knowledge that I now had of him. This, together with the appreciation of being able to walk out in the fresh air without panic attacks, shopping alone at the supermarket and being able to sleep at night without the fear of feeling that I was going to die, made me grateful and mindful not to take these everyday activities for granted.

Chapter 7

> But when he, the spirit of truth, comes, he will guide you into all truth.
>
> John Ch 16 v 13

I could look back and see that God's hand had been upon me at all times. Even when I had not understood what was happening, God was working out his purposes and plans for me. This gave me a greater confidence in his sovereignty. I continued to desire to be open to his teachings, knowing that in general, man does not think in God's way. We have to seek his way with an act of our will, coming against all that would hinder. God did not expect me to know everything, but little by little as he revealed the truth to me by the Holy Spirit, he did expect me to acknowledge that truth. Precept upon precept the knowledge of God was given to me to help me walk his way, yet even that knowledge itself was not something to be grasped at and made my own. It was brought to remembrance by the same Holy Spirit who revealed it to me originally, confirming teachings and prompting their use, allowing me to test the spirit of new teachings and be aware of the deceptive work of the enemy. My God had made himself real to me and in a very personal way. He was a lamp unto my feet showing me where to make my next step.

I had come to the conclusion that a Christian could have the influence of a demon upon or within them, but this did not mean demon possession. It does mean that at times there can be a block in a relationship with God. Lack of knowledge in this area, in the light of the Holy Spirit, can cause its own problems. I realised that God's answer to anything that hindered me was to consistently be open to the Holy Spirit and to let him deal with it in his way. Many scriptures were making sense to me concerning Jesus' position over the works of the enemy.

He had said of himself in John Ch 14 v 6 that he was "The way, the truth and the life" and as the Holy Spirit had been given to us to direct the way and guide us in all truth, I could see that this truth was – the knowing more about Jesus.

This is confirmed 1 John Ch 8 v 32 which refers to knowing the truth, and this setting me free, and John Ch 8 v 36: "So if the son sets you free, you shall be free indeed."

This revelation of Jesus blessed me, and my own experiences had confirmed the revelation in that the truth is A PERSON, who can relate to me, NOW. Being set free seemed to be an ongoing work though. As I read of the enemy being described as, "The thief who comes to steal, kill and destroy" in John Ch 10 v 10 that and experiencing him coming to try and do just that.

However the other half of that scripture is where Jesus says,"I have come that they may have life and have it to the full." This full life is not how the world would see it, but very much concerned with my relationship with Jesus and walking in the light that is revealed by The Holy Spirit.

I knew that there was nothing in the world that could offer more fullness of joy than the knowledge of hearing God and being obedient and seeing him at work in my life, or in the lives of those around me. In 1 John Ch 4 v 4 it is said, "He that is in me is greater than he that is in the world" and I knew this to be true.

However because the enemy is known as the "father of lies" and can work very subtly, the walk is often difficult. This knowledge made me aware also of the constant battle within myself that sometimes caused me to fall short of fulfilling my desire to walk in obedience.

The Lord continued to bless and encourage me in this though, as he is faithful to forgive our confessed sins. I could not blame the devil for my own failures, but in Psalm Ch 37 v 23-24 I am continually uplifted as I read, "The Lord delights in the way of the man whose steps he has made firm. Though he stumble he will not fall for The Lord upholds him with his hand."

I knew how real this was in my life and thanked God for upholding me. In 1 John Ch 3 v 8 it states, "The reason the Son of God appeared was to destroy the Devil's works." I wanted to work with God in this and my prayer life had become very important to me. When Margaret had been with me, she had encouraged me to pray along with her audibly in tongues or in my own understanding. I was not quite sure about this, as previously I had prayed only quietly if someone else was praying out loud. She explained that by doing so, it did things in the Spiritual Realms and encouraged her too. I did what she asked me, but but I also asked The Lord to confirm his ways to me regarding such matters.

We had just welcomed a new Pastor to our fellowship, a man of God who radiated The Lord's presence that caused my spirit to trust him. At our first prayer meeting with him I was pleased to hear that he prayed with ease in the way that Margaret had previously suggested. I thanked God for this confirmation and enjoyed the freedom of this powerful way of praying.

I was moved in compassion to want to pray for and with Janet, a lady from our fellowship. I had been obedient to such prompting in the past and knew The Lord's blessing on such occasions. I made myself available to Janet and she agreed to meet with me. We opened ourselves to The Lord and both witnessed to the fact that The Lord had brought us together for a purpose as yet not revealed. We were both willing to meet together weekly, seeking The Lord's purposes, and praying together in a deeper way. Quite quickly we were blessed with the gift of Maralyn, a mature Christian, who came alongside us, teaching us from her own experiences as we prayed together.

It was revealed to us that we must pray for the town and for the Body of Christ, that is every believer in the town. We also prayed for each other and experienced God's care and love for one another.

These times were really special to me and taught me more practically in intercession. Sometimes we would touch God's heart and feel very sad and troubled. At other times we would burst with joy as we witnessed in our spirits that the Lord had heard our prayers and was answering us. Occasionally we would pray as though we were in a battle against the enemy, proclaiming scriptural truths and speaking out into the spiritual realm just like Jesus had done when he had rebuked Satan in the wilderness.

After a while Marilyn moved out of the area. She had helped us to lay down foundations of intercession and spiritual warfare that we would use in future as the Spirit led. I thanked God for the valuable times that we shared together.

All of the above experience had not just helped me with my walk with God, but also assisted in my ministry to others which I still found a joy to do as God directed me. I could still just talk to my Heavenly Father about things that concerned me and my personal bible study brought such blessing. It was good to apply scriptures to myself in prayer.

During the same period of time I was meeting with four ladies who lived in nearby streets for fellowship, sharing problems, care and prayer. We were all from different backgrounds of worship but it was good to share our common ground in Jesus Christ and have our views of the Body of Christ widened. One of the ladies, Janet, was married to Stephen who was the curate of the nearby Anglican church. He called to see me one day and was very interested in the subject of Spiritual Warfare in Prayer. I loaned him a book that I had just read as he informed me that he was scheduled to speak about prayer at the Inter Denominational renewal meeting in the town. I promised to be there to support him and did attend.

I thought that he talked well on the subject until he mentioned the Authority of God, which he quickly passed over, admitting that it was something that he had not grasped at that time. I later talked with his wife, Janet, and offered to look out every scripture on the subject of God's Authority for him. I never actually did this. I did research the scriptures. I read them out to John, then I read them out to my two friends Gem and Ann. I thought that I knew them, but it was only as I read them over for the third time that the revelation of the truth of them hit me.

By the grace of God, I HAD THIS AUTHORITY. I just wanted to shout for joy and dance. I praised The Lord and thanked him, knowing that he wanted me to understand them for myself. He could reveal these things to Stephen at another time, his perfect time.

This proved to me, yet again, that I needed to receive these truths deeper than in just my mind. This revelation was to help me to be even more free to pray as The Holy Spirit led me.

My children in their own ways had made commitments to The Lord Jesus. Even though they are normal boys I had had the pleasure of seeing glimpses of their faith in action, and I had no doubt that Jesus was real to them. In May 1986, when Philip was 7 years old, the school nurse encouraged me to take him to the optician to have his eyesight checked. We already had a routine appointment there with Neil the next day, and a quick telephone call ensured that we could take Philip along too, believing that it would be no more than a routine check for him also. To my surprise, the optician informed us that there was something in Philip's right eye, and he advised John and I to take him to our GP. I was not too concerned about this until a letter arrived from the optician the very next day emphasising that we took Philip to the doctor as soon as possible. The Doctor referred us to the Hospital Consultant eye surgeon, and within a short time we saw him. By this time

I was concerned about the urgency and had been praying. The consultant informed me that Philip had a moderately serious eye condition, which after a number of tests, he hoped to be able to treat. Philip was rather proud that he was the only boy in the whole of Darlington to have this condition. The name given was Uveitis, inflammation within the eye which could cause destruction of this sensitive organ.

We were sent to Leeds Infirmary for a second opinion and were informed of the many side effects of the use of steroids which was the chosen treatment. There was no definite answers for the future for Philip so the fellowship joined us with our prayers for his healing.

Shortly after we had been informed of the seriousness of Philip's eye condition, a visiting Evangelist to the fellowship was inviting people forward for prayer. I took Philip forward for prayer for healing. To my surprise the Minister did not pray for healing but spoke over Philip with a Prophetic Word.(A gift of the Spirit speaking to us as if God himself was speaking into the situation).

Basically, he said that this problem was in The Lord's hands and that Philip would lead many to Jesus. I wrote it down in my bible and dated it 30th November 1986. It proved a comfort to me through some traumatic times that were to lie ahead. Philip was able to pray for himself, read his own bible, and knew every story about Jesus healing blind men, and so remained confident that Jesus would heal him, in his time and in his way.

The scriptures recorded many different ways in which blind men received their sight. This encouraged me personally for I knew that nothing was impossible with God, and that he did not keep to a set pattern to answer prayer, even if man tried to keep him to one. John and I wanted to keep open to the Holy Spirit's promptings concerning Philip, no matter what else was said to us. This did not mean that we did not receive help or listen to the doctors. We went along with every suggestion unless within our spirits we believed that we had to speak out.

My own experiences concerning God's sovereignty and timings had allowed me to move from questions of "Why?" when problems arose, to "What do you want me to do in this situation Lord?"

I had a growing confidence that God could and would direct me specifically in any situation yet I remained sensitive to others opinions of faith in action which could cause self condemnation.

One day I was sat talking to my Heavenly Father trying to explore why I was so sensitive to how others thought that I should express faith. I was prompted to look at Paul's life through Acts of the Apostles, the Epistles of Paul to the churches, and any commentaries that I had in order to research his character. I recorded the following observations:

Paul's life was abandoned to The Lord. He knew the miraculous upon his own life and he knew deliverance from prison, all according to God's purposes and glory. Also to God's glory Paul knew sicknesses upon his body and imprisonment for the gospel's sake. Paul was shown how to glorify God in every situation, and he encouraged others not to be ashamed of such things for they were indeed used to further the gospel. He even stopped other Christians from holding him back from being in chains because he knew what the Holy Spirit wanted personally of him. Paul's total sufficiency was God, and he willingly trusted God and abandoned himself to him. He neither demanded miracles nor release from his chains.

These revelations blessed me and in whatever God had for me in the future, I wanted to be as abandoned as Paul was to God. They gave me peace and knowledge that the Holy Spirit himself had ministered to me. Confirmation of these revelations came as Pastor Steve encouraged the whole fellowship to abandon themselves to The Lord. I found his teachings, in general, anointed of God, real and practical, and I recognised that we had been given a marvellous gift in Pastor Steve.

My desire to be fruitful in the service of God caused me to meditate on the 15th Chapter of John's Gospel where it is expressed that Jesus is the vine and we are the branches. To bear much fruit I had to be prepared to be pruned. I was willing for this and as I prayed John 15 over my life, I specifically said "Father I want to be wide open to you, so that you can see what needs to be cut off me. Like a surgeon takes a knife, so you too cut away all that is not of you and would cause me harm."

The Lord had heard my prayer and I looked forward to the unfolding of his answer.

Chapter 8

> For I know that through your prayers and help given by the Spirit of Jesus Christ, what has happened to me will turn out for my deliverance.
>
> Philippians 1 v19

My latest blood results showed that I was low on iron yet again. Now that was free from panic attacks, I agreed this time to have further investigations carried out at the hospital. The night before I was due to have the camera put down into my stomach (gastroscopy) I was in some pain. I had realised that my health was not too good in general and that there must be something wrong to give the pain, but whatever it was I hoped that that it could be treated. I specifically prayed that if there was something in my stomach that the doctors would not overlook it.

Much prayer had been carried out for me by my many friends and at the weekly church prayer meeting. I had not looked forward to this particular investigation when I realised that I would be awake during it, but now that I was on the operating table I knew God's presence with me and I was not afraid at all. I watched everything that the doctors had to do to me. I said, "Praise The Lord!" as soon as it was over as there had been no trouble.

An injection of valium had been given to me to make me "feel nice" rather than a total anaesthetic. I was seen by a doctor before leaving the hospital. He asked me how my stomach felt. I told him that I was in pain at the moment. He told me that he was not surprised as they had observed that my stomach was inflamed and they also believed that I had Coeliac Disease (malabsorption problem caused by an intolerance to gluten in wheat). I was surprised to hear that as I thought that it was only diagnosed in babies. He told me that they were not certain about the diagnosis but would be able to tell me more when they had the biopsy result in two weeks time. I was prescribed some pills for my stomach and allowed to go home.

The consultant's secretary rang me at home a couple of days prior to my appointment to hear the biopsy result. She said that she was making certain that I was going to keep the appointment. I questioned the reason for her telephone call. She told me that it was just routine and nothing to worry about. As this had never happened before, I suspected that there was some bad news to come. I knew that Coeliac Disease was bad news because it would mean a complete change of diet and that I would have to give up many of my favourite foods.

I took John along with me for moral support. I left him in the waiting room and went in to the consultant alone. Coeliac disease was confirmed and satisfied my own thoughts about an absorption problem being the reason for the anaemia in the first place. The consultant then shocked me as he told me that he wanted to pass me on to a surgeon as they had found what he called a "pre cancerous condition" in my stomach. He seemed uneasy as he tried to tell me that if I had been 67 years old he might have expected to find it, but as I was only 37 years old, it had not been expected by any of the medical professionals who had dealings with me. He seemed pleased that I believed in God in the way that I did. In that instant, I was glad that the investigations had been carried out and that the problem had not been missed. This answered my prayer on the night before the procedure was carried out.

But, cancer or pre-cancerous? What was I to say to John? I could imagine how he would feel as the word cancer would be the furthest thing from his mind. As we waited to see the dietician I related to John all that the doctor had told me, which really wasn't much. We joked nervously over the idea of no more Yorkshire puddings or lovely fresh crusts of bread. Suddenly the new diet did not matter to me now, I had a bigger concern to think about.

Upon arriving home I contacted a couple of close friends and informed them of what I had been told. The word Cancer brought questions from them to which I had no answers. I spent the rest of the evening sitting quietly with John.

That night I slept well. I woke to hear myself singing the words of a hymn: "Because he lives I can face tomorrow." I realised that it was my spirit singing and I rejoiced in the truth of it.

The medical consultant's secretary rang me that day to tell me that she had made an appointment for me to see the surgeon the following week. I told her that I could not keep that appointment as we were going to a church conference at Bognor Regis all that week. She impressed upon me the urgency of seeing the surgeon and said that she would ring back. She rang back with an appointment prior to our departure to Bognor. All of this activity made me uneasy and I checked with John at the Police Office to ensure that he would be able to attend with me to hear for himself what the surgeon had to say.

Sitting on my own in prayer, I started to cry. It was not for myself but for my children. I knew the problems that had beset my two younger sisters without a mother, and I did not want to die until my boys were grown up. I openly made my request known to The Lord and the number 92 came into my mind. My bible was on my knee and I opened it up at Psalm 92 (Amplified Version Verses 12 – 15) and read these words:

> The uncompromisingly righteous shall flourish like the palm tree - be long lived, stately, upright, useful and fruitful; he shall grow like a cedar in Lebanon (they shall flourish in the courts of our God. Growing in grace, they shall still bring forth fruit in old age; they shall be full of sap (of spiritual vitality) and rich in verdure of trust, love and contentment); they are living memorials to show that The Lord is upright and faithful to his promises; he is my rock and there is no unrighteousness in him.
>
> Psalm Ch 92 v 12-15 (AMP)

I did not need to ask God again. I realised in that moment that I would see my children grow up and be able to take care of themselves. Peace flowed over me. This was not just a hope; I had asked God specifically and he had answered just as specifically. I believed it and lived in the truth of it.

I had to check with my GP about prescriptions needed to enable me to have special food for my new diet. As I was seeing the surgeon the next day and had peace about the life or death question, I had not expected to discuss my stomach problem with her. Not knowing what I had been told at the hospital, my GP thought that she was giving me words of comfort when she she said that I could be cured by having my stomach removed. This shocked me and I asked what life would be like without a stomach. I really did not want to think about that kind of answer, and I suggested that I might have a miracle instead. To me, a miracle did not seem out of the question.

When I got home, I was quick to get before The Lord and ask what he thought about me having my stomach removed. My choice of reading for that day had been Paul's letter to the Philippians. As I started to read the first chapter, I knew that God was again speaking to me specifically and in Verse 20 I received his peace with these words (Amplified Version):

> This is in keeping with my own eager desire and persistent expectation and hope, that I shall not disgrace myself nor be put to shame in anything; but that with the utmost freedom of speech and unfailing courage, now as always heretofore, Christ the Messiah, will be magnified and get glory and praise in this body of mine and be boldly exalted, whether through life or through death.
>
> Philippians Ch 1 v 20 (AMP)

I was satisfied that God had answered me yet again, and that I was with him and He was with me. I would not disgrace myself or be put to shame and God would get the glory. I believed that The Lord was asking me to trust the circumstances to him, and at that moment, I could.

Next day at the hospital the surgeon carried out an examination, asked a few questions and then said he would like me to come into hospital for surgery the following week. Well, I was not about to do that as I had already said I was going to conference with my family and I told the surgeon this. I questioned the need for the urgency. He was quick and to the point in his reply, that I had an early cancer and that he needed to remove it. I was pleased that it had been found early, as from my nursing experience I knew that this problem carried a poor prognosis as it was usually found too late. I was however a little annoyed that the first consultant had not been totally open with me.

On reflection, it must be difficult for a doctor with little knowledge of a patient to know exactly what to say in such circumstances. When he heard that I was not prepared to come in, he agreed to see me the following week with the choice of doing everything necessary on that occasion or for him to look into the stomach for himself, take further biopsies and discuss his findings with me before any surgery. I opted for the second choice as I preferred to know every detail about medical matters. I also thought that if God worked a miracle at a conference among so many believers, the cancer would be gone when the surgeon looked into my stomach with the camera tube. I told him my thoughts and I am sure that he would have been delighted if that had proved to be the case. I was bold or foolish to say that I belonged to The Lord Jesus, that He was my authority and that the surgeon could not touch me unless God allowed him to. The surgeon answered in a way that truly blessed me by saying that his hands were given to God to be used to heal. I really liked that. It felt good in my spirit, but the idea of pain was not so good. I had not really accepted it and had pushed it to the back of my mind and desired a miracle instead.

On the way home, we called at Pastor's home. At our request, he prayed over John and me as we both tried to come to terms with what had been said at the hospital. That night we told our children that I did have a serious problem but reminded them that we knew the person with all of the answers. We shared the scriptures that God had given to me and prayed together asking God for His answers and the possibility of receiving a miracle whilst at the conference. I did not mention the need for surgery to them at that time as I was desiring a miracle. I thought that to talk about surgery would amount to a lack of faith on my part. I did not want to hinder any answers from God by accepting that surgery was inevitable.

The boys did not show any worries over what I had told them. I believe that they were more taken up with plans for going to Bognor Regis the next day. The conference takes place within Butlins Holiday Camp and is a fun packed week for the children, so their mother's illness was not a priority for them. It is very usual for me to have difficulty in sleeping when in a strange bed, so Maralyn had agreed to intercede for me for the whole week whilst I was away. I really felt the benefit of these prayers as I slept well, in fact much better than on previous visits to Bognor. I was pleased that we had not cancelled our plans to be there as there is something very exciting about worshipping the Lord with thousands of Christians.

I met with old friends and enlisted their prayer support for my condition together with their love and care as we shared in fellowship. The teaching seminars were very interesting, a great deal being centred on God's miraculous healing powers at work today. I believed that I was open to receive a miracle and at times, God's presence with me was so tangible.

In previous years there had been opportunities for anyone to walk forward and have ministers pray over them for healing, but this year it was kept to Leaders calling individuals to the front under the power of The Holy Spirit. My prayer prior to going to Bognor was that I would be called out in such a manner for healing, but it did not happen. In one of the seminars on prayer, we had been encouraged to pray over each other in small groups, and I was blessed when a total stranger confirmed previous ministry when she prayed over me. I also received many confirmations of previous teachings and new revelation on spiritual warfare.

Towards the end of the week a mature lady was allowed to speak from the platform about her recent experiences. I listened very carefully as she disclosed that she had been diagnosed as having an inoperable cancer of the pancreas. When the doctors had operated and found that they could do nothing for her she had been quite elated at the thought of soon meeting face to face with Jesus. The elation had concerned the doctors as they tried to explain that she was about to die. She had understood all right and was pleased that she would be going to heaven because of her faith in Jesus. She had been offered chemotherapy to prolong her life a little, and because of pressure from her family she had accepted it. The chemotherapy had made her very unwell and weak but she had not lost her joy and she was looking forward to a dream come true as she had planned to go to Israel.

Despite being ill in hospital, she did go on the trip and had enough energy to keep up with the others in the party on the long walks in the rugged countryside. This had surprised everyone and she had given all the glory to God as she believed that it had been his special blessing to her.

After her holiday she had carried on with the chemotherapy and again became so ill that the doctors had to stop the treatment. Instead of getting worse, she actually got better. When they examined her again the doctors could find no cancer. Strangely enough, when told this, she had cried as she realised that she would not die soon and go to heaven. God spoke into the situation and told her that he wanted her to go and tell everybody about what had happened to her to God's own glory. It was not time for her to die yet, and there she was, doing exactly that.

On hearing this story, I found it strange to reconcile it with the teachings of that week on the miraculous. The testimony was full of God's anointing and I believed that God was trying to speak to me. I did not want to go through operations, then chemotherapy and then get well. I wanted God to glorify himself by giving me a miracle first and I continued to pray for the cancer cells to disappear. I did not have a "Gift of faith" for such a miracle, just a hope. I had gifts of faith about things in the past, and I did know the difference. At that time, I was requesting a miracle because I did not want surgery and I was doing all that I could to stand with that request.

Whilst still at conference I met Pastor Steve, and when he heard that I had not been called to the front for healing, he suggested that the situation be shared with the whole fellowship when we returned home to enlist their prayer support.

The week that we were at conference coincided with a “Europe Against Cancer Week” on the television. Each lunchtime in our chalet I watched programmes about cancer victims and their experiences. As I watched, I was very moved by some of the tragic stories that were told. The main problems appeared to be a feeling of being placed under a death sentence, fear of pain, fear of the unknown and not being able to speak the word – cancer. It was as if it had some power of its own.

I did not believe that I had any of these difficulties apart from thinking of the pain of surgery. It made me see how much God was with me and, that in my relationship with him, I did not have to face any problem alone.

I had slept well. I knew that I was not going to die yet, and I could say the word – cancer easily because I knew that the name of Jesus was higher than any other name, including that of cancer. I was filled with compassion for the people shown on the television and countless others who must suffer in the same way. I wanted to help others not to be afraid and prayed that God would allow me to do so in the future.

Chapter 9

> But he knows that way that I take. When he has tested me I shall come forth as gold.
>
> Job Ch 23 v 10

On Sunday 29th April 1988 I spoke to the whole fellowship about my condition and asked them to stand with me in the two scriptures that The Lord had given to me: Psalm Ch 92 expressing fruitful life, and Philippians Ch 1 v 20 expressing that God would be glorified.

Pastor Steve encouraged those who felt it right to come forward and to stand and pray with me. Nearly everyone got out of their seats, surrounded me and prayed. I cried with a joy for the love that was shared that morning, and for the support of the body, and the individual prayers that were anointed of God. It is an experience that will stay with me forever. It is a privilege to belong to such a fellowship who were not afraid to share my problems and show to me their love.

Between that Sunday and Wednesday, when I was due to go to hospital, different friends called to see me and express their own sorrow at the shock of hearing about the diagnosis of cancer. I was at peace. My visitors were not, and it was I who encouraged them about the future. I could understand their feelings. They were on the outside looking in and wondering or knowing how they would feel if the roles were reversed. They were also wondering if I would survive or if would they be losing me. I was in the trial and I had God's grace for it, they did not have that grace nor the trial. This was a revelation to me of how one can have peace in the middle of a storm. The fact that I had God's grace meant that, in many cases, I was stronger than my friends, but it was really special to feel their care and love for me.

I spent the whole of the Wednesday at the hospital. I had to have a general anaesthetic and the whole experience had not been as easy for me as the first gastroscopy had been. The young American doctor in attendance could only express her sorrow for the wait and inconvenience I had suffered. I was pleased when that day was over.

I later spoke to Pastor Steve about his own understanding of what the Lord was doing in my situation. I was still hoping for a miracle, and now that the second biopsies had been taken I could only wait to see whether my prayers would be answered in that way. Pastor Steve told me that God had informed him of the serious nature of the problem before I had even known about it. The knowledge had been given to him by God in order that he could pray in the spirit for me.

With the prompting of The Holy Spirit he had prayed two prayers: "May her life be spared," and "May God be glorified." I immediately reflected on the two scriptures that I had been given and realised that they were a direct answer to Pastor Steve's prayers. There was no guarantee of a miracle. Whilst bathing, I considered all the implications of faith, miracles, healing, glorifying God and I could see that I could make my request known. God could answer with a miracle according to his purposes, or he could answer with healing that does not look miraculous but which is according to his plans and purpose that I am not seeing at the moment. I knew that I could not think Miracle, Miracle, Miracle and shut myself off from God's purposes.

The story of Lazarus came to mind. He had actually died before The Lord was glorified. It had been promised in John Ch 11 v 4 that God was going to get glory through Lazarus, but it had not come according to the expectations of others. Jesus had wanted Mary to trust in Him and not the circumstances. When Lazarus was brought back to life, more people put their faith in Jesus than would have done with a healing prior to his death. I realised that God was asking me to trust him and surrender the problem to him. I did just that and asked God to glorify himself in his way. Peace was upon me even if it meant surgery.

It seemed an age for the ten days to pass for the biopsy result. I asked the Lord if he could let me know if surgery was inevitable in order that I could prepare the children for the event. In answer, the next day a letter came from the hospital. It simply stated that an ulcer and inflammation had been found and the surgeon looked forward to seeing me at the clinic. This confused me because it did not mention malignancy. I wondered whether the diagnosis had changed. I made an urgent appointment with my GP to discuss this. I found out that this was typical of this surgeon to leave out such words as malignant and cancer in such letters, and that the diagnosis of cancer of the stomach had not changed.

I thanked God for his answer as I could now prepare John and the children to expect the surgery, direct the prayers of the fellowship in a more positive way and receive their practical support if necessary. I met Pastor Steve at a function that same evening and related the latest news to him and made a request for family prayers. I asked that it be related to the prayer meeting on the following evening to which he agreed. I don't know what had happened in the meantime, but when the prayer meeting was held, Pastor requested everyone to stand around me and petition The Lord for a miracle. I felt like Jesus must have felt when he said to Peter, "Get thee behind me Satan." I was not at peace with these prayers because I had made my requests known as prompted by The Lord.

When everyone had finished praying I spoke out to explain that whatever would be seen in the future they should not be surprised. God was going to be glorified in his way for his purposes. I left the meeting quite upset as things had not gone as I thought that they would. I called at my friend Ann's house on the way home. I was glad she was in. She understood me and comforted me as I wept.

Shortly after, Pastor did let me know that he had felt the change in the spirit but could do nothing at that time. He publicly spoke out about it the following week and requested prayer to support John and the children. He explained that he had hoped for a miracle so that I would not have to suffer, and that is how others also felt. I had felt the same, but I knew God's way forward for me.

The following Sunday, Harry (one of our Deacons) told me he had been praying for me and had received this word from The Lord for me: "You will not be cut down like the grass or be blown away like the chaff. You will grow as the poppy and bloom and people will know that you are mine."

This really was a confirming word in what God was saying in my spirit and to a word given to me by Maralyn that same week. It was a scripture: "But he knows the way that I take. When he has tested me I shall come forth as gold." (Job Ch 23 v 10)

When I next talked with the surgeon we discussed an admission date for the operation. I asked him about the spread of the cancer and how much of my stomach he would have to remove. He answered me by basically saying that he would cut out all that would cause me harm. I had prayed for the surgeon since our first meeting so I felt that, in God, I could trust his words. I remembered back to the prayer that I had made about the vine and the branches, especially the part, "like a surgeon takes a knife, so you too cut away all that is not of you and would cause me harm."

What a way to answer that prayer! I knew that God had a sense of humour, but I did not expect him to take me so literally, and I told him so. I could see that the answer was a real one. The cancer had been uncovered and had to be cut out. My Father God did care for me and He is my healer. I could trust him and I was ready to go into hospital.

Before going into hospital I had to let the rest of the family know. Margaret, in New Zealand, had known from the outset and I had her prayer support. Each member of John's family was informed, and although it was a shock to them, it was an easy task to do. My family was a totally different proposition. My mother had died from cancer, and to inform dad that I had cancer would prove a burden to him. He was already under pressure helping my brother Peter with his invalid wife, and helping my youngest sister Christine who now had three young children. Christine was now divorced and had suffered further psychotic episodes. Maureen's husband had been medically retired and she had problems.

With all of these things in mind, I decided not to tell them until I was out of hospital and recuperating, and I would tell them I had been operated on for an ulcer. John arranged for two weeks holiday and the boys were looking forward to helping him to run the house whilst I was away.

Chapter 10

> They will run and not grow weary, they will walk and not faint.
>
> Isaiah Ch 40 v 31

I was admitted into the hospital, ready to submit to the rules, regulations and restrictions of a surgical ward. After the doctor had taken a history and examined me, he asked if I had any worries that might hinder my recovery from surgery. I could honestly tell him, at that time, that I did not relish the thoughts of pain but I was at peace, my trust was in God, and I would get through it all with his help.

It was as if I was being tested upon my remarks to the doctor when, a couple of hours later, whilst looking out of the window, a feeling of fear came over me. Thoughts of never actually being the same again, the pain of surgery and the fear of anaesthetics just hit me. The only other person in the room was an old lady, and as she was asleep, I started to pray in tongues and ask The Lord to help me to overcome this feeling. It reminded me of panic attacks that I had not suffered for two years now, and I was certainly not going to accept a recurrence of them now.

I paced up and down, praying as I felt my heart race, missing beats at times, my breathing uneasy as I stood against it. Within a few minutes it was gone, just as quickly as it had come. I believed it had been a work of the enemy to try and rob me of my peace in God. Pastor Steve came to see me. I talked to him about this and he prayed with me against any future recurrence.

Despite being at peace, the first night brought my old problem of not being able to sleep in a strange bed. However a friend of mine was on duty on the ward that night and plied me with conversation and cups of tea throughout the night. I saw this as another provision of God's blessing. Another acquaintance of mine was on duty on the Intensive Care Unit and paid me a visit. I had been told that depending on the particular procedure chosen by the surgeon, I could spend a couple of days in intensive care, so it was good to know that I knew one of the nurses who would be on duty there too.

Throughout the next day, friends visited and communicated their support. I felt encouraged and blessed. The morning of the operation arrived, and as I was first on the list, I was soon prepared for theatre. I was taken to the anaesthetic room and just as the anaesthetist prepared to give me an injection, I committed myself into God's hands. The anaesthetist said "Just a scratch," and the next thing I remembered was waking up in the intensive care unit.

I had a tube up my nose and an oxygen mask on my face. I could not move even if I tried. It was six o'clock at night and I had lost 10 hours in time. As I looked around I could see wires attached to my chest to monitor my heart, an intravenous drip in my arm, a large tube with a clamp coming out of my chest, and another large tube coming out of my abdomen on the other side of my body. I also had a catheter fitted. I praised God for the catheter as it precluded the use of a bedpan. I did not feel much pain as I was on constant intravenous pain relief. I just had the feeling that I had lost the use of my muscles and felt pinned to the bed.

John arrived wearing an apron, the uniform of the intensive care unit. The surgical registrar also arrived and described to both of us what had happened in theatre. They had removed approximately half of my stomach, a couple of inches of my oesophagus (gullet or food pipe) and my spleen. The procedure had necessitated the collapse of my left lung and the opening of my rib cage to reach to the end of my stomach and oesophagus. This was the reason that I had an underwater seal drainage tube coming from my chest cavity and also the reason why I had to be the subject of intensive care. Wow!

I was pleased that I had not known the full details before the operation, as such knowledge may have interfered with my peace. It was later found that the glands around the stomach were free from cancer, proving again that the cancer had been found early. The prognosis was good.

John had some news for me from my sister Maureen. I was not expecting to be in contact with her until I was recovered. It was bad news. Her husband, Brian, who had poor eyesight had stepped out in front of a vehicle and was now in

Middlesbrough General Hospital having been critically injured. Obviously I could not help at all. I just prayed that her finding out that I too was in intensive care would not cause her more problems. It felt very dark as I thought of the possibility of Brian dying, but all I could do was give it over to God in prayer.

There had been no other patients in intensive care during my stay there, so I was definitely well looked after. It was a shock to my system when I was returned to the busy ward. I felt extremely ill. Two doctors were in attendance on me, and after some discussion between them, a number of different drugs were added to my attached infusion line into my vein.

As these doctors left me, two nurses wanted to help me out of bed to have a walk. I really did realise the need for quick post-operative mobility, but I was in shock at the move from intensive care, and I would have preferred to have been left for a short while. I believe that I was looked upon as a reluctant patient and was bullied to my feet. I just wanted to recover for a little longer, but I soon found out that routine was routine for the good of the ward, and we had not to struggle against it. I don't know how my body moved or succeeded in that walk. I just shut my eyes and prayed that I would not fall to the ground so giving me more problems. I was told that all patients coming from intensive care were the same – SPOILED!

I think that the problem lay with the fact that patients may be more ill when they came from intensive care, but I was in no position to argue. I remember thinking to myself that if I ever took up nursing again, I would have more compassion for and even empathy with patients.

With the various drugs that I was given came headaches and hallucinations. If I refused the drugs the pain became unbearable. Before going into hospital I had contacted BACUP (British Association of Cancer United Patients) to obtain information. I had received a book which had described what to expect after operation. It explained that the nasogastric tube and drainage tube would be removed after 48 hours, after which sips of water could be taken. As I had spent 48 hours in intensive care I was encouraged to think that any discomfort was now feeling would soon be reduced. I would then be able to cope with more visitors including the children. Up until now only John and Pastor Steve had visited me.

Visitors did arrive on the Sunday, four full days after operation. I still had every tube, drip and drain attached to me. I was totally exhausted all of the time as the discomfort prevented me from sleeping. I could not cope with the visitors and asked John to explain this to various people who wished to visit, and that he would let them know when I was up to receiving visitors. One day moved into the next, and after seven days I could see no way forward. I had not even had one sip of water and the drain from my chest cavity caused me extreme pain. I imagined the pain to be like that of pleurisy.

When I talked with Dr Kathy, the young American doctor, she agreed. The drain would be irritating the membranes around the lung causing inflammation. I felt that I could stand no more of it and told Pastor Steve that I knew the bible said that God only allows us what we can bear. At that moment, I doubted that God knew me at all, as I could stand no more. Pastor Steve's prayers for me at that time did nothing to comfort me. In fact I could feel nothing of the presence of God. I just felt ill, inadequate and empty. God had promised that he would glorify himself. I could not understand how he could get any glory with me in such a state of disrepair.

That evening as the doctors were making their routine ward round, I was promised that the drain from my chest would be removed the next day as X-rays had proved that my lung was sufficiently recovered. I reflected on this good news coming right at the moment of my cry of despair. Although I had to go through one more night of discomfort, the news truly lifted my spirit. The next day Dr Kathy and another House Officer prepared me for the removal of the drain from my chest. They told me that although the procedure was simple, it did have its complications.

Being afraid at this time would not help as it was essential for me to be completely still. I asked for them to wait a moment whilst I rebuked fear in the name of Jesus. Then, with peace upon me and trust in God that there would be no complications, I allowed them to carry on. It is difficult to express the relief from the specific pain and discomfort that I felt immediately after that drain was removed.

From that time on I needed no more strong painkillers, so allowing my head to clear. That was a really good day, so different from the previous one. I could smile again and take notice of and converse with those around me. More time was needed before the abdominal drain could be removed, but that was nothing compared to the chest drain. I could walk on my own now, pushing the drip stand with one hand and carrying the drainage bag in the other. As the catheter had been removed too, I could manoeuvre myself to the loo and back. FREEDOM!

During the previous seven days when two nurses had to take me for my routine walk with bottles, bags and drip stand, I would quote Isaiah Ch 40 v 31 under my breath: “I shall mount up on eagles wings, I will run and not be weary, I will walk and not be faint." On one occasion, feeling more faint than usual owing to an extended walk, I must have spoken the scripture a little louder, and one of the nurses had asked me what I was doing. I told her that I was quoting scripture to help keep me upright. She laughed but it must have made some impression, as later, one of my visitors, who knew other staff in the hospital, had questioned me about the incident. The nurses had been talking about it amongst themselves and my visitor expected that it was me they were talking about. This made me smile.

I had to have physiotherapy every day following the operation, and I found that one of the physiotherapists shared my faith, together with a couple of the nurses and one of the dieticians. I had to see my dietician, Yvonne, quite often, and she supported me in prayer as well as helping me in her professional capacity. I really appreciated this blessing from God.

A couple of other nurses were quite curious about my faith in Jesus and I was only too pleased to answer their questions. One night Dr Kathy was talking to a group of us about being afraid of anaesthetics herself, confirming that doctors and nurses make the worst patients. She knew that I had been a nurse in the past and wanted to express that I had not fallen into that category. She referred back to our first meeting in the Day Ward some six weeks earlier. She remembered, she said, because she had noticed something about me, a presence of strength and peace. She remarked that it had remained with me all the way through my ordeal. I asked her whether she knew that I believed in someone much bigger than myself, and she stated that she believed that was what she was seeing in me.

I was very blessed with these comments because I could give glory to God that they had been made. I had received an answer to my question: “How could God receive any glory while I was so weak? I had been unable to feel his presence with me, yet he had allowed this doctor to see it, and to tell me about it. This made an impression upon me, knowing that he had been with me in a real way all of the time.

My stay in hospital was for nearly three weeks. The surgeon wanted me to stay longer to see if I improved in my attempts to eat. However, my eldest son Neil had been complaining of being unwell, and with John having returned to work, I wanted to be at home for Neil. He was only 11 years old. Even though I could do nothing physically for Neil, the surgeon understood my concern and discharged me. Neil remained unwell for quite some time with various symptoms of headache, stomach ache and joint pains. I suspected that he was worried about me although he would not admit it. Later on when I was recovered, Neil did admit that when he had visited me in hospital and had seen all the tubes and how I looked, he had thought that I was going to die. Daniel was also shocked at that time but recovered quickly. Philip was never concerned about such things, he was just sad for me if I was in pain.

As I left hospital I had over 60 cards, some poems and some lovely letters of encouragement for which I was very grateful. I thanked God for every blessing received in this way.

Chapter 11

> I am The Lord who heals you
>
> Exodus Ch15v26

Now that I was home I thought that I would recover quickly, but I was mistaken. There was a constant battle between having to eat without an appetite because my body needed it, and the pain and discomfort that came when I did eat. An added problem was that food would stick in the oesophagus no matter how much care I had taken in chewing it. This brought a totally different pain as the oesophagus tried to push against the food that was stuck. I was sure that all of these things would settle down in time, but I had a couple of frightening moments and then watched God intervene in the circumstances.

On one occasion, just a few days after being discharged, I decided that I could do a little bit of tidying up after the boys had gone out to school. I started to feel strange so I laid down on the settee until a friend knocked at our front door. As I got up to answer the door I realised that I had done too much, and that I had been silly for trying. My friend Eileen, made me a cup of tea while I laid down on the settee again.

As I got up to answer another knock at the door I could hardly stand. It was my friend Ann. She had previously arranged to come and do the ironing for me. By this time, Ann observed that my breathing was funny and my colour strange. She decided that she would go upstairs and clean as my distressed condition had upset her. I believed that I needed to eat something sweet, so Eileen got me a biscuit. I felt very unwell and prayed that it would soon pass.

As I did so, Pastor Steve arrived just in time to give me spiritual ministry as I felt that I would pass out. When he saw my distress he put his hand on my abdomen and started to pray. I felt his touch, lay into the cushions and soaked up the blessings. I saw Pastor take his hand off my abdomen and yet there was a distinct feeling that hand was still there. I started to feel much better. Ann told me that my colour was much improved.

Eileen had by this time left, so the three of us started to chat together. I asked Pastor whether he thought there was a spiritual block on my part in receiving God's blessing because I could so easily become so unwell. He said that there was no block, only the enemy trying to rob me of the blessing. He said that God was even in charge of that, and that the enemy could only come so near. He went on to say that whilst he was praying The Lord had caused him to see in the spirit, Jesus himself come and put his hand on my abdomen, and he was not about to take it off. My experience as Steve prayed proved the truth of this. Again God was speaking to me personally of his sovereignty and his specific care for me. God had his purposes in all that was happening to me and I could praise him. I also promised Ann that I would not try to tidy up again until I was much stronger. She was relieved to hear my promise.

One morning the following week I got up and vomited continuously. I felt that I could not even take a drink. Even the thought of trying made me nauseated. I knew how much my body needed energy and I tried to force myself to eat. This just made matters worse. Weak and frustrated I rang Maralyn to seek her prayer support. She admitted that as she thought that I had improved, she had not been praying as much for me. She committed herself to pray for me that morning. I gave up on trying to get sustenance into my body and just retired to bed. With my eyes shut, I was wondering whether I would experience good health again, when a light seemed to go on. It was like the sun coming out from behind a cloud and shining brightly. I felt the presence of The Lord and an almost audible voice said to me, "I am The Lord that heals you." I replied, "Yes you are." I felt strengthened and I remember thinking he does not have to work a miracle. HE WAS HEALING ME.

I had a drink and laid down again. I was alone in the house and said to The Lord, "I know that I can eat now, but I do not feel strong enough to get up and make myself something."

At that moment I heard a tapping at the window. It was Janet, the Anglican Curate's wife. I beckoned her to come in and found that she had brought me some pureed vegetables just ready to eat. I thanked her and told her that she was an answer to prayer. I ate the food without any problem and it strengthened me. This again was God's blessing and I knew the success of Maralyn's prayer, standing against the enemy for me.

I made steady progress as my wounds healed and my strength increased, but I was to have two more stays in hospital before my eating improved. The join between my oesophagus and my stomach was too tight and the surgeon had to carry out two small procedures to stretch it in a similar manner to a gastroscopy. This meant a two day stay in hospital on each occasion, but the benefits were enormous.

In the meantime, Philip's eye condition and its treatment were giving me cause for concern. Initially high doses of oral steroids were given to bring the problem under control. Once control had been achieved, just a small dose of steroid was required to maintain the effect. This had proved successful, and for at least a year, all was well with Philip. A higher dose was again now required, so I wanted to discuss with the surgeon any other method of treatment.

It was possible to inject steroids into Philip's eye under a general anaesthetic. I had shied away from this method in the past because I had a problem with the thought of my own children receiving anaesthetics. The surgeon claimed some personal success with this method and so we agreed to give it a try. It was time for me to pray about my reason for anxiety about my children and anaesthetics.

There was no secret as far as I could understand, just facts. Whilst I was a trainee nurse I had witnessed a two year old boy come very close to death as he choked whilst recovering from an anaesthetic. I just saw how easily this could occur. My first baby, Paula died shortly after the administration of an anaesthetic, and whilst I knew that heart failure was the cause of her death, because I was not with her at the time I had visions of her choking to death after the anaesthetic.

When my other children had gone for small operations this had always been at the foremost of my mind and I would not settle until they had fully recovered. I put all of these thoughts before The Lord and asked him to deal with me. I shut my eyes and sat quietly. In my mind, I pictured Paula in a cot in a room. Into that room came what I can only say must have been the Lord Jesus. I saw this figure come up to the cot and pick up the very peaceful looking baby in his arms. It was not as if I was just imagining this, it was like watching the television and I was wondering what would happen next.

This figure held Paula so gently and was saying to me that Paula had not choked or struggled, but that He had come to take her home. I was being ministered to and counselled by the Holy Spirit. I gently wept and received healing. I was able to take Philip to hospital as many times as was necessary without anxiety. Praise God, I was free.

I had become involved in the work that God had for me quite quickly after the operation as people called to see me and we would pray together. By the time that four months had passed I was even more active in the work, with enthusiasm, strength and energy, enjoying life to the full. My stomach and eating habits did continue to give me problems but with the grace of God operating within me this did not interfere with my renewed joy of living and working for Jesus.

There were many aspects of my improved health that could be attributed to the gluten free diet. Instead of it being a problem to me, I could really appreciate it and gave God the glory. These benefits were that I did not become anaemic thereby eliminating the need to take iron pills with all of the associated problems. Everyone commented on my skin looking clearer. I had a long history of skin problems and my GP had been ready to send me to see a dermatologist before I commenced the diet. My weight was about one stone lighter than my average weight prior to surgery. This was quite a shock to some people, but they soon got used to it, especially when I purchased new clothes to fit.

My relationship with my Lord was even deeper because of my experiences. I looked forward to helping in a very real way the people who God would bring to me.

Chapter 12

> And he sees the sword coming against the land and blows the trumpet to warn the people.
>
> Ezekiel Ch 33 v 3

When I was discharged from hospital I made contact with my family in Hartlepool by telephone. My brother, Peter, was the easiest to talk to about the diagnosis of cancer and the subsequent surgery. He expressed disappointment about not being told earlier. As we talked and I explained my reasons for not informing them, he understood and realised that I had wanted to protect the family from further stress until I was well.

I found out from Maureen that Brian had not been expected to live at first after his accident. However whilst he had been unconscious Brian believed that he was visited by God and had spoken into his situation. This had made a big impression on Brian which was still evident when I spoke to him on the telephone. Maureen confirmed that something had happened as the doctors were amazed at Brian's recovery from his injuries with very little noticeable damage to his brain.

Brian had also spent three weeks in hospital. Both Maureen and Dad had been up for most of the first evening praying to God, and they were delighted to give God the glory for Brian's recovery. Brian suffered from cataracts making his eyesight very poor. Sadly since the accident, he did not feel safe at home, therefore Maureen had given up her job to look after him.

My sister Christine had been well for a few months and her three children had been returned to her from foster care by Social Services. Christine had committed her life to Jesus, and in answer to a prayer of mine, The Lord had provided some Christian friends to support her in her difficulties.

I spoke to dad a few times on the telephone, and although he was pleased to hear my voice, I was aware that he was still worried about me. I planned to visit him with John and the children. I thought that when dad actually saw me his worries would be allayed and he would know that I was alright.

By the time that we actually made the visit more problems had arisen for Christine. She was back in hospital in the psychiatric unit and her children had been returned to their foster parents. Peter's wife had also been quite ill, so I knew that dad would be under some stress. He was pleased to see me and the children. After initial greetings dad and I discussed my situation. He of course brought up my mother's own death from cancer. I was able to say that my situation was very different. I shared with him the promises that I had received from God. Although he had not liked my moving from the

Roman Catholic Church, he knew that my faith was real. He had seen God working in my life and he was happy to accept that I really did believe those promises.

I felt satisfied that my dad was happy with being able to see that I was all right, but it was not to be the case later. My brother Peter rang me to share some serious news about his wife. She was in kidney failure, had pneumonia and had suffered four cardiac arrests in the previous twenty four hours. Peter had been told by the medical staff that she was about to die, and that if he wanted anyone to visit, now was the time. I was shocked with the news and very sad for Peter. John and I made arrangements to visit the hospital intensive care ward. When we arrived she was unconscious, so we sat with Peter in a waiting room before I actually saw her. Peter talked about his own desires to see his wife come through this ordeal, yet death seemed so imminent.

As I talked with Peter I was aware that he was more open to my talking about my faith in Jesus. He was facing death and he was seeking an answer from God. He knew it was his only hope. My confidence in God, and the reasoning that I could give Peter for this confidence, was enhanced by my recent experience of having to face life or death. Peter listened and was prepared to make a pact with God. He was prepared to commit his own life to God in order to see his wife's life spared. He was honest enough to tell me that if his wife lived he would probably forget serving God as his time would be taken up with looking to her needs again. He allowed me to pray with him. This was a First.

I walked into the intensive care unit and saw Peter's wife with the look of death upon her. In my own nursing experiences I had not seen anyone look that close to death and survive. A machine was breathing for her, fever was upon her body and her kidneys had failed. She was not strong enough to be put on a dialysis machine and the diabetes she had could not be controlled. As I stood there I wondered whether she knew Jesus. I was very aware of what it says in Ezekiel Ch 33 v 1-11, where it expresses to me that it is my duty to tell someone about Jesus taking the punishment for their sins. It is especially so if I know that their death may be soon and that I must somehow warn them if I am able. If I do not do this then I myself will stand responsible before God. If the warning is not heeded to repent from sin and turn to Jesus, then it is not my problem.

I had never had a previous opportunity to talk to her about Jesus. Peter knew how much my faith in Jesus helped me, but he had not wanted me to embarrass anybody. Now I asked God for an opportunity. I looked at her body and literally felt an anger rise up in me against death. I rebuked it in Jesus name and prayed that God would give her back to Peter at that time. Prior to leaving, Peter told me that I had done an unselfish act. He believed that if his wife died he would have time to seek God, but if she lived as I had prayed he might not have time to seek God. At that moment in time I was more concerned with his wife's salvation. Peter was already warming to the real truth about Jesus and I believed that God could deal with him later.

I talked openly with Peter about my concerns about dad. Dad had been involved in Peter's struggles with his wife being so ill, and in supporting and visiting Christine in hospital over the last few months. Dad was also a great support to Brian. I noticed that Dad seemed to be under stress. He was a man of great strength of character. I respected him as he always seemed to surmount problems easily, but now I could see the strain upon him, and I was concerned. Peter informed me that dad could cope with all of these things and that it was I who was the cause of his stress. He explained that because dad had only found out about me being in hospital by chance, because of Brian's accident, he now believed that I would easily keep the truth of my condition from him. He could not trust what I told him. The possibility of me dying and him not being able to do anything was the cause of his worry and strained look.

Well! I had unwittingly caused dad more problems than I had tried to keep from him. We left the hospital and went to visit dad. I tried to explain yet again the reason for keeping the news of my condition from him in the first place. Now that he knew about the cancer, everything that we had told him was true, and at that moment in time I was all right and expected to remain so. I could not make him believe me and I was a little sad for him and all the problems with the family.

The next day Bill was leading the Sunday morning church service. He asked for anyone with prayer requests to come forward and the elders would pray. I went to the front and related the situations at Hartlepool. His response was to ask for the whole congregation to stand in prayer with us. That afternoon I rang Peter at the hospital He was absolutely full of praises to God. The doctors had expected death and yet they had witnessed for themselves a miraculous change in Peter's wife. She was now off the respirator, her temperature was normal and dialysis had been given. Moreover, there was no brain damage resulting from the cardiac arrests and the doctors had told Peter, “God has done this work.”

Peter believed it, and so did my dad. Of course, I agreed with them. It was the beginning of December when this happened and Peter was able to take his wife home for Christmas. Peter was determined to do something for God but as his wife remained weak and in need of his help, as expected he did not have the time. I was prompted to write to his wife about Jesus. I thanked God for the opportunity. She read this inspired letter of testimony with Peter. He encouraged her by saying that there was definitely something in what I had to say. I was now at peace about warning Peter's wife about forgiveness of sins before she died.

Peter enjoyed her company for a further six months. She developed gangrene in her feet and a slow painful death was predicted. Peter was now ready to let her go. He rang me on the same day that the doctor gave him the sad news. We prayed that The Lord would undertake and have mercy upon her so that she would not suffer. That afternoon she went into a diabetic coma and died. We could praise God for his mercy. She was 38 years old.

Peter came to stay with us for a short while. He could see that God had been with him in his grief and could sense the presence of God in my home. He came to church with me, and although he was not prepared to commit himself to God yet, he was seeking the truth and I knew that God was revealing himself to him.

Chapter 13

> Let us hold unswervingly to the hope we profess, for he who promised is faithful.
>
> Hebrews Ch 10 v23

I have shared in a previous chapter how The Lord had confirmed that he was with us in the difficulties surrounding Philip's eye problem. I expected God's guidance therefore that meant that I had to pray about every suggested manner of treatment. I had to trust that God would indeed reveal his purposes and guidance.

Every time that I had concerns I received prayer support from the fellowship, for which I thank God. I did feel uneasy at times, particularly when Philip showed side effects to the treatment. I had overcome the fear of anaesthetics for Philip. I was pleased to see that the first injection had not caused him too much suffering.

For my part, it was easier to have the drug given in this way rather than orally as it had been for the previous two and a half years. The consultant eye surgeon's report on the first injection was favourable and he hoped that it would be effective for at least a couple of months, however he wanted to combine it with the continued use of oral steroids. I had hoped that Philip could have discontinued using the tablets. I started to seek The Lord on this issue and asked friends to pray that I would receive wisdom.

I came across the address of a medical information centre in London that sent out written information on medical matters. I contacted them by telephone as I desired to receive as much information as possible about the effects of long term use of steroids on the body in order to make an informed decision. I found their information to be very balanced. They also encouraged me to send details of Philip's eye problem to them in order for their consultant eye surgeon to tell whether there was any known alternative treatment. I decided to write to them. It wasn't that I did not trust Philip's consultant, on the contrary, I found him to be an excellent man. I was just curious. I received a quick reply from London which sadly stated that in cases like Philip had, steroids was the recommended treatment until there was nothing left to treat. In other words, steroids themselves held no guarantee of curing the problem.

After much prayer and discussion with John, I felt right to ask that Philip be taken off the tablets. I sought my GP's support first. She agreed to contact the consultant before our next appointment with him. The consultant was happy to go along with our wishes, and only further eye injections were given when necessary.

As the effect of the tablets wore off, Philip's left eye began to show signs of disease and an injection was administered into that eye also. I was not too concerned about this as I had the feeling that Philip would get worse before he actually got better. It was good to see Philip looking well in general. Six months later Philip started to complain about difficulty with school work as black dots intermittently obscured his vision. One night he complained of thumping sensation inside his left eye. The next morning he asked me to fasten his school tie for him as he could not see sufficiently in the mirror to do it for himself.

On questioning him further, I found that he could see nothing out of his left eye and that he was relying on his already poor sight in his right eye. I petitioned The Lord again for direction and received peace about Philip having to go back onto oral steroids. Next day at the hospital we were informed that Philip had haemorrhaged into his left eye, totally blocking his sight. It was necessary to commence a very high dose of steroids to save his sight and he had to be admitted for observations whilst his body settled to the treatment.

The consultant carried out some painful examinations upon Philip's eyes, making them water. As we sat in the waiting room prior to going to the ward I suspected that he was crying a little too. He had never been an in patient before. I held him close to me and really felt God's touch upon us as the words of a song was on my lips. I spoke them gently: “He is here, he is here, he is moving among us.”

At that point, one of the receptionists, whom we had become familiar with, came across to talk to Philip. She promised that she would visit him next morning before commencing her duties. This cheered Philip and made him more determined to make the best of his stay in hospital. I knew that God would reveal his glory some how, I just had to trust him. Philip stayed on the ward until the following weekend when we were allowed to take him home before returning him at 8am on Monday morning.

When we returned to the hospital further tests were carried out. Upon completion we were given an appointment to see a Professor the next day at Newcastle Royal Victoria Infirmary. We were told to be prepared for Philip to be admitted to that hospital if necessary. This caused Philip to be a little apprehensive about being so far away from home as regards visiting. I did not fancy driving up and down to Newcastle personally, so I contacted John at the Police Office and related all of the latest news. I praised God that John was able to take holiday for one week immediately. I must say that through all of the difficulties, the supervisors of the police force have always given us the care and support with holidays at short notice and time off when necessary. This has been a real help to us as a family.

Whilst John, Philip and I were travelling up to Newcastle, I shared with Philip about my own experiences of being a patient in a Newcastle hospital when I was a child. I had fond memories even though my my family could not visit me because of lack of transport.

Philip's consultant was seeking a second opinion from the Professor about the cause of the haemorrhage and the subsequent long term treatment with steroids and additional drugs. The Professor confirmed that steroids was the best choice of treatment and a balance had to be achieved between successful treatment and risk of side effects. He said that because sight was a very important sense, he would make the saving of it his priority. I told him that we knew about the serious side effects of long term use of steroids and that we would prefer to err on the side of general health. I did not desire that Philip would end up with more problems.

He expressed that we could not have our son's best interest at heart and he gave us many examples of sight being lost by parents making wrong decisions. I was not going against medical advice at this time, but I did tell him that we believed in Jesus and that He would direct us in the future when necessary. I was sure that Jesus had our son's best interest at heart. I held on to the promise that God was with us in this situation as I tried to overcome the Professor's remarks. I was encouraged by John as he witnessed that I had not got upset as I had put my case forward. I thanked him for his encouragement.

Philip was admitted to the eye ward as steroid treatment had caused sugar to be present in his urine and diabetes had to be ruled out. Other examinations and investigations also had to be carried out. Another doctor was in charge of him on the ward and it was not necessary to see the Professor again. Philip was rather quiet and seemed upset about his admission. I sat him on my knee and had to fight my own tears as I tried to comfort him. I asked him if anything in particular was upsetting him.

He said he was concerned about not being able to have visitors. He had taken my own story as me telling him that he would be left on his own without visitors. I had only been trying to encourage him and I cleared up the misunderstanding. We had a car, and of course we would be visiting him. He felt better and we were able to inform him that Ann's daughter,

Michelle, who was studying at Newcastle would also be in to visit him.

His hospital stay lasted for five days. When he returned home it was obvious that the treatment was affecting him. He was easily exhausted, he suffered mood swings and his appetite was increased. The sight in his right eye was improved slightly by the provision of spectacles. He had not worn spectacles before.

He wanted to return to school, so we talked to the teachers to make them aware of his difficulties. We received their support. He returned to school to find that the children had been collecting money to buy a present for him. Now that he had returned to school prior to the present being purchased, it was decided to let Philip donate the money to a school charity of his choosing. This was a lovely idea and Philip really appreciated the other children's thoughts for him.

By this time, Philip's features were changing dramatically, and with his new spectacles he was not easily recognisable. This brought some negative responses from some children in name calling and finger pointing. I was very proud in the way that Philip dealt with this and praised God for Philip's personality.

When two months had passed and there was no sign of Philip ever coming off the drugs, I started to fret a little, partly because the negative side effects were constantly seen in the way that Philip looked. I used to think that Philip was in there somewhere, but it was difficult to see his true features. When I had Philip with me, people would sometimes ask where he was and be quite visibly shocked when I pointed to him.

Prayer support at that time was great, probably because the problems could easily be seen. On most Sundays, individuals would petition God to heal Philip. I was seeking God continuously, wondering if I had missed a direction somewhere. I would question John as to whether he was seeking God's answers and challenged him in the process. It was easy for me to put myself under condemnation, especially when Philip's situation was not improving.

Back under the supervision of the Darlington consultant we agreed to introduce a new drug that would enable a reduction in steroids without losing the effect. It meant that Philip had to have another five day stay in hospital, but he was quite pleased as he was used to hospital routine now. Philip had to have regular blood checks with taking the new drug, but he was very brave and didn't mind. We seemed to be making some progress. He could see slightly with his left eye, but this caused more problems as the eye itself did not focus anymore and gave Philip double vision.

At one of the subsequent check up appointments the consultant could give no guarantee that the double vision and focusing would ever improve. Then when he looked into the right eye, he called another consultant into the room. They both looked at Philip's eyes and then talked together. I could tell that things were serious. The consultant confirmed this when he told me that the retina in the right eye was oozing, causing a bleb to appear. He wanted us to take Philip to St Thomas' Hospital in London to which we agreed.

Our next appointment with the consultant was in two weeks. During that time everything seemed to go wrong in my ministry and in relationships so I sat up one night and poured out my troubles to The Lord. I asked God if he was actually going to allow Philip to lose his sight completely before he intervened. Even though Philip had talked about the possibility of losing his sight previously, it was only now that it was real to him and he was upset. I cried to The Lord for mercy and ensured that I had done all that God had asked of me. I surrendered the whole situation again into God's hands.

That weekend, John was to sing at a meeting in town where a well known man of God was leading a healing meeting. I asked Philip if he would let me take him along to the meeting to see whether God would use this man to heal his eyes. Philip did not want to go with me. He preferred to watch television instead. I felt upset about this and the whole situation. I tried again to persuade him to come to the meeting, and very reluctantly, he agreed.

At the meeting no one actually prayed over Philip but God's presence moved over me. I asked God for mercy and surrendered Philip to him yet again. On the way home Philip was still annoyed at me for taking him to the meeting. He commented on the fact that no one had prayed over him. However within a couple of days Philip's left eye began to focus and double vision disappeared. We were both excited when we next saw the consultant. We did not have to say a word about it as he could see the difference immediately. On closer examination the consultant got quite excited and said, “It’s a miracle, better than waving a magic wand.”

He had just prepared the long letter to go down to London and he encouraged us still to go, even though the situation had improved. I asked him about the serious condition in the right eye. He apologised for not mentioning it. He had not read his notes from the previous appointment. He read them, looked into Philip's right eye again and then told us that the bleb had gone. I was continuously praising God openly, and even the nurses joined in the enthusiasm. That was a good day.

That evening I shared the news at the prayer meeting. God spoke in a prophetic message to the effect that he had started the healing and that he would finish it. We kept the London hospital appointment at a much later date. By that time the consultant there could only see a very small problem. He encouraged the Darlington consultant to take Philip off his drugs slowly. That has now happened, although the drugs were reduced very slowly. Philip continued to improve, and today as I write some eighteen months later, Philip has good eyesight and needs no medication or spectacles.

The Lord is faithful to his promises.

God let me know that when there was no direction from him, it was because he was not saying anything new. I had fretted a little for no reason. It proves again that the enemy works even harder to keep us from the promised victory. Philip continues to have check ups at the hospital. The consultant is pleased to agree that miracle did take place. As a family we say, "To God be the glory."

Chapter 14

> These have come so that your faith - of greater worth than gold which perishes even though refined by fire - may be proved genuine and may result in praise, glory and honour when Jesus Christ is revealed.
>
> Peter Ch 1 v7

As I willingly moved into a deeper knowledge of God, I was very aware of the revelation of his blessings to me, in and through every trial. These blessings of God's love and care for me as an individual sometimes overwhelmed me. This was especially so when my private petitions were answered in an open way for all to see. Many would comment on God's special love for me as they watched God answer so many prayers specifically. I saw this as God being faithful to his word. For example Psalm Ch 37 v 4: "Delight yourself in The Lord and he will give you the desires of your heart."

I was beginning to see that I did want to be obedient to God in such a real way that it was a delight to seek him. As I committed myself to him and his plans it was he who put the desires there in the first instance. I found it easy to seek God on behalf of those that he had me care for, and pray that certain desires would be fulfilled for them. It was a little harder for me to pray for God to allow me to do something that would benefit myself as well as others. I had to be especially sure that it was in God's plans and not just because I willed it. This was very true of a growing desire to visit my sister Margaret in New Zealand again, and also to visit my uncle and his family in Australia.

This being so, in January 1989 I prayed that God would know that I desired to be obedient to him more than to make the trip. I gave God total permission to either confirm the trip or show me how he would have me use the savings that we already had, which we intended as a start towards the airfares. In other words I was prepared to save hard and yet give money away as he directed. I wanted God's confirmation and I was expressing this to John one day as I had my bible open at 2 Corinthians Ch 9. The chapter was talking about being ready to give to others in need, sowing generously and therefore reaping generously, so that every good work can be done. That God himself would supply all of our needs, and thanks to God would be made because of our generosity.

In verse 9 John saw that the scripture said, “He has scattered abroad...” and he said that it confirmed to him that as we give as God tells us to give, we would go ABROAD on this desired trip. This made me laugh as John had taken the scripture totally out of context, yet, as I looked at the whole chapter again, I realised that our finances belonged to God anyway, and that he would direct us in our giving. We were prompted on a few occasions to give specifically in certain areas above our normal tithe, and God was faithful to bless us according to his purposes.

One blessing came in the form of a short midweek break in a caravan in Norfolk. John had used up his holiday time whilst Philip had been in hospital and we were not expecting to take a holiday. We were now saving hard to pay for the proposed trip to New Zealand in April 1990. So the offer of Maralyn's caravan was special. Marilyn had moved to Norwich and because of our recent trials over Philip's eyesight problem she had wanted to bless us. It was a great time, the weather was beautiful and it refreshed us all. It was also good to have fellowship with Marilyn and her family again.

As we were planning to take up Marilyn's offer of the use of the caravan, our need for a larger car became obvious. This was not just for the Norfolk trip, but the even longer run to the airport with all the luggage for a round the world holiday. We had previously looked at larger cars knowing that we had a growing family and that we would outgrow our present car. Our financial situation dictated that we would have to wait until after we had visited Margaret. We had seen a new car launched that we had liked the look of, and we had in mind to purchase at the later date.

One day we met Eileen at the supermarket. She was keen to tell us that good quality skirts were in a sale at a shop in town and encouraged John to think about buying me one. As we had recently looked at our financial affairs we believed that all of our money was spoken for, and that it was probably not wise to go to the sales. Later, after some discussion, John and I decide that there was no harm in taking a look at these so called "good bargains." We had to pass the garage that sold the model of the new car that we had in mind to change to. There on the forecourt was the first one to be part exchanged by its first owner, making the price of the car very attractive. We never did get to see the skirts as I felt the promptings of the Holy Spirit to believe that we should purchase this car.

Having had a test drive, we were sat discussing finance with the salesman when we became aware of people almost standing in line desiring to purchase the same car. We felt that it confirmed in the Lord that we could have it, so we had no hesitation in agreeing to buy it. It was just what we needed to travel down to Norfolk. We gave thanks to God for going ahead of us and showing us the way, meeting our every need.

I did miss Maralyn and the spiritual giftings that were in use through her. Janet and I had continued to grow in The Lord together, but it had been good that God confirmed his ways to us through Maralyn. I was talking to Pastor Steve about the need for God to give me someone else to lead me on in The Lord. I knew that Steve had every ability. The Holy Spirit moved through him, a mighty teaching ministry backed by practical experience, but he was too busy to spend time with me personally. He knew what I was meaning, and encouraged me by saying that I was allowed to ask God for such a person. I had been doing exactly that. I expected that the answer would be in another "mature" Christian joining our fellowship. God answered me, but not in the way that I had expected.

Janet had told me about a friend of hers who was warming to the gospel message. We had prayed together for her on a couple of occasions. It was good to see her come to the church and eventually become a "Born again" Christian as she committed her life to Jesus. As the months went by, I became more involved in praying for her and I watched her grow in her sensitivity in hearing The Lord.

One day after I had been struggling to know what God was expecting of me in a sensitive area of ministry, this lady rang me. She explained nervously that God had asked her to say some words to me from him. Those words, I could confirm to her, were a direct answer to the dilemma that I was in. This lady's name was Sue. Sue had no personal knowledge of the reasons for speaking to me in the way that she did, but I was able to tell her that the Holy Spirit had spoken through her to answer my prayer.

It became evident to me that God desired me to get alongside Sue in a way that would allow him to teach her and encourage her in the things of God. I found that by The Spirit of God working through her, she was the answer to my prayer to have the gap filled that Maralyn's move had created. This was something of a revelation to me. I had looked for a mature christian, but God had given me a baby christian. I had looked for someone who had more knowledge of God than I had, but God answered by giving me a person who was available and open to God to be used.

She had no preconceived ideas about how God could or should work. She had no prior knowledge of religion before her conversion, therefore she was a perfect channel for God to use as he desired. This proved to me again to me how God will use all those who make themselves available to him. He can use educated men who know the bible well, or he can use the youngest christian, but in either case they must be available to him. God can speak to each one of us. We must believe that he can do this and surrender unto him. I thank

God for the "Sues" of these days who hear God and who are obedient.

The simple truths, revelations, teachings and confirmations that I have received through God's gifts to me in his obedient servants cannot be put into words to sufficiently show my appreciation. I can only say, "Thank you God for meeting my needs through your obedient children and all glory goes to you as I see you move through them."

Margaret and her family were informed of our proposal to visit them again. My own motivation for the visit was to thank her husband Peter for allowing her to come over to see me in the past. I also wanted to bless Margaret by allowing her to see that I was well after my operation for stomach cancer. She and her fellowship had prayed much on my behalf and I felt that it would be good to let them see the results of their prayers. Margaret had just moved into a larger house so accommodation was no problem. Her children were looking forward to getting to know my boys better.

Uncle Frank and Auntie Rene in Australia were also looking forward to seeing us again. We had previously met them about three years earlier when they had visited England. At that time they had invited us to visit them. Uncle Frank had four sons and a daughter who we had never met, so there was a lot to achieve in the eight days that we had planned to spend with them. We also intended to spend at least three days in Los Angeles to see Disneyland for the second time (first time for Daniel) and to see Universal Studios that we had heard so much about.

With seven months still to go before our planned date to travel we went around all of the local travel agents seeking the best deal. The difference in some of the prices was unbelievable. Having done the trip twice before, we knew which airlines to choose and the type of hotel for our stay in Los Angeles.

As we were quite specific in what we required we were offered a certain promotion which, if we took it up immediately, would give us a £500 saving on the next price quoted. Sadly our money was in the Post Office and would take one month to be released. There was no guarantee that the special offer would still be available then. We would just have to wait and see. In the meantime we put the waiting time to good use by arranging John's leave to be taken all together which required special permission.

I also needed a letter from my GP stating her approval and listing both mine and Philip's medical history for travel insurance purposes. My GP was willing to give her permission as she could see how well I was. In fact, I had only consulted with her on one occasion in the last nine months. She was genuinely pleased that I was well and referred to Philip's situation as a possible problem. I had already asked Philip's consultant, and he had said to go ahead with the trip, and so we were able to collect the required letter.

With three weeks to wait before we could have the money to pay for the air tickets, I sat before the Lord and talked about the possibility of the price remaining the same. I just knew God's blessing on the situation. I cannot explain how I knew, I just did. Three weeks passed and it was confirmed to us that the price had not changed. On 4th October 1989 bookings were made to travel on 1st April 1990 to Los Angeles for three days, New Zealand for four and a half weeks and Australia for eight days.

We were so blessed as a family. Philip's eyes were on the mend and we were looking forward to a fantastic holiday sealed in God's blessings. The price of the tickets enabled us to have more spending money available too. As weeks went by and the tickets arrived, I was pleased that I had looked so well when requesting the doctor's approval to travel.

Now however, I was a little concerned for my health as I could feel a lump in my abdomen. At first I thought that it was attached to my intestines, and cancer came to my mind. Whilst I had been in hospital I had seen patients come in for investigations of the intestine and the necessary preparations caused them serious discomfort. With that in mind, I just hoped that, whatever the lump was, it would just go away of its own accord.

After ten days I could still feel the lump and additional symptoms made me feel that it was connected with my womb. This was an easier thing for me to think about as I felt that it could be a benign growth of fibroids. John was upset. I knew that he was just expecting cancer again. I had believed that I had been cured with the operation and thanked God for it. I was not believing it was cancer on this occasion. I was sad for John and asked everyone to pray for him. I asked to see my GP and was able to have an appointment that same evening. I asked her for her opinion as she examined my abdomen but she would not commit herself, preferring to refer me to the gynaecologist at the hospital. My GP felt that investigations might be needed before a diagnosis could be made.

I received an appointment for the hospital in the following week. Before attending the hospital I was in prayer with Sue who spoke to me in a prophetic word. I wrote it down in my bible and dated it 10th November 1989: "The Lord declares I will go to New Zealand and I will be well. I go in his name."

The Lord's confirmation of the trip coming again at this time gave me confidence to believe that the problem was a simple one. With these thoughts in mind as I went to the hospital I was quite prepared to say to the consultant that if an operation was necessary could it wait till after my holiday. The consultant would not commit himself to an opinion but stated that he wanted to carry out a hysterectomy. Casually asked him if I was to be put on a waiting list as I would be out of the country the following April.

I soon got an idea of what he thought he was dealing with as he informed me that he wished to operate the following week. He told me that the operation would allow the surgeon who had operated on my stomach to check me over to make sure that no other organs were involved.

The same night I sat before The Lord reading the scripture in 1 Peter Ch1 which talks about trials and God's glory, and I thought, "How appropriate." I was sure that I was going on the trip to New Zealand and the scriptures were talking about faith being tested. I was at peace. I was not going to go through any thoughts of being miraculously cured this time as I was strong enough to trust the whole situation into God's hands. I went to the prayer meeting at church the following evening and I requested prayer for John. Pastor Steve's chosen scripture for the evening was taken from 1 Peter Ch 1. I knew God's confirming ways. I was not afraid, and as the time came nearer to go into hospital God was revealing more of himself to me. I tried to explain this revelation to Janet but it caused her problems. I was truly understanding that my life was totally given over to God and that if I lived or died, it would be in his purposes... FREEDOM...

Peace was upon me in a powerful way. As I talked with Janet she thought that I meant that I wanted to die. It was not like that. It was God's control of death itself that made me see that no petitioning of God would help me keep life for any longer than he had planned for me.

I visited Pastor Steve on the night before I was due into hospital because I had heard that he was unwell and I wanted to pray for him. We talked at length about the Lord's ways of revealing himself in our lives and I nervously outlined my latest revelation of life and death. He really understood and that felt good to me.

On my way up to the ward I called to see Yvonne my dietician to confirm my admission and allow her to make preparation for the special needs of my diet. I knew that she would visit with me on the ward and I looked forward to those visits. She was also prepared to commit herself to pray for me over the issue of pain of surgery, and this was a bonus. I was ready for another hospital stay, wondering how God would bring about his promises. I was not afraid of pain, cancer or death. God's presence felt very close and I looked forward to his opportunities.

Chapter 15

> And we have the word of the prophets made more certain. And you will do well to pay attention to it, as to a light shining in a dark place, until the day dawns and the morning star rises in your heart.
>
> Peter 1 v19

I was admitted to hospital on Wednesday 22nd November 1989. My surgery was planned for the following Friday. The gynaecologist was to perform a hysterectomy and the surgeon who had carried out my stomach operation was going to assist in order to check out my abdominal cavity for any other organ involvement. Having had so many other hospital admissions I was not anxious at all. In fact I was mildly excited to see how God was going to bring about all of his promises. There was also a possibility to meet up with and renew my acquaintance with many of the nurses, and to meet others.

There was another lady waiting to follow the admission procedures at the same time and she was expecting to undergo a similar operation. She was very nervous and I warmed to her. I desired to help her overcome her anxiety. She was very easy to talk to and we soon felt as if we had known each other all of our lives. Her name was Judi. We were to be in the same six bedded room so it was easy to be at one with each other in the days ahead. I cannot possibly talk to anyone for a long period of time without expressing my faith in Jesus and how he has spoken to me through the bible. Talking to Judi was no exception, so from that first hour she knew where my trust lay.

My first interview with the House Officer brought to light that the growth in my abdomen was not totally solid and was possibly outside of the womb. My thoughts that the growth may be something like fibroids were now gone. I felt the Lord was preparing the way for me to accept that this was indeed to be another battle with cancer. I was still at peace for myself. My prayers were for John to be able to be ready to accept the diagnosis when all of the facts were known. As the procedure for surgery was explained to me, I was told that I could possibly retain one of my ovaries depending on what was found. I made a mental note that if my ovaries were removed that it would also be an indication of malignancy to me.

As Judi and I settled in, we were introduced to the other patients in the room. A lady in the next bed had rosary beads hanging on her bedhead and religious pictures around her. We were soon in conversation about religion, faith in God and opinions of how to express such things. Other patients joined in this conversation and it became quite interesting to hear that not one of them believed that there was no God. How real he was to them as individuals showed up the difference between religious behaviour and personal knowledge of God. With my bible on view to all, I made no secret of my living relationship with The Lord Jesus. The lady in the next bed with the beads made it obvious that such thoughts and beliefs should be kept private. I did not desire to offend her and was ready to respect her wishes, but Judi explained that she could see a reality in me about this relationship, and wanted to know more.

The next morning Judi told me of a dream that she had in the night in which she was told to have me read Psalm 27 to her and explain its meaning. Because the dream had been so real to her, she insisted that I actually would do it. I was blessed at the thought and was quite excited to agree to her wishes. I knew that the Holy Spirit was at work. I picked up my bible and started to walk towards Judi's bed. The religious lady in the next bed to me called out, "You're not going to convert her are you?" I replied "No, I'm not, God is." I believed this to be true. Judi did not know The Lord for herself and had expressed some personal fears the previous day. The Psalm contained many answers to these fears. I was very aware of The Lord's presence and Judi was truly amazed. She could not believe that it was just a coincidence – I knew it wasn't.

I was first on the list for operation that Friday morning. I was soon prepared ready to go into theatre. I knew that I would not suffer the intensity of pain that I had suffered after my stomach operation. I was totally at peace as I committed my life to the Lord yet again. I experienced again that unusual feeling of waking up on the ward, operation completed, yet feeling that no time had passed.

This time I had an intravenous drip in my arm but very little discomfort in my abdomen. I remembered that Yvonne was going to pray specifically against pain. Everything in my body seemed so easy so I thanked The Lord for answering her prayers.

As the Nursing Sister washed me and put me back into my nightdress I asked if my ovaries were still with me. The answer was negative. This confirmed to me that cancer had been found again. I had a relatively comfortable night and the gynaecologist visited me the next day. He explained that it had been the ovaries that had been affected but the full implications would not be known until biopsy results were to hand. This meant a few more days waiting for the total picture to emerge.

Judi became quite ill and the doctors did not seem to know the reason. I was able to get up and about so I asked if I could pray with her. She agreed and as prayed quietly I felt it right just to hold Judi and rock her gently. As I rocked her she informed me that her mother would have held her in just the same way had she still been alive. He mother had died some years previously and Judi still missed her. This was another touch of God's hand upon this relationship. After a couple of days she was taken into a side ward for special care whilst I was moved to another six bedded ward. I was pleased to be allowed to continue to visit her and help her get through.

Whilst visiting Judi I recognised another lady in another side ward. She had been in the first six bedded room with me. She was old, seriously ill and had not slept for many nights. I talked with her and found that she loved Jesus and asked that I read some special bible verses to comfort her. That of course was a privilege and a pleasure to do. Before leaving her room I prayed that she would sleep well that night. The next morning the nurses informed me that they had not needed to do much for her in the night as she had slept through. When I visited her later that day she told me that she believed that God had sent me to her and that he had met with us together. This really blessed me.

Again as I visited Judi, she said that she didn't believe that I'd been in for an operation at all, but God had sent me into hospital to comfort her in her trial. This really made me laugh, but I was quite sad to see Judi so poorly.

The stay in hospital seemed to be blessed for me at every point except eating the hospital food, hence I had many visits from the dieticians, Yvonne and Sandra. I also had visits from Pastor Steve, the church elders and many friends.

In the new area that I had been moved to I met up with two other ladies, both called Pauline, who helped to pass the time away in humour and with stories. I still remain in touch with them.

Even when the gynaecologist arrived to tell me the full story of their findings I was at peace. He had talked to all of the other patients openly. My bed was the last on the ward, and as he approached the nurses started to draw the curtains. He sat himself on the bed and took my hand but it was I that spoke first. I said, “It’s cancer, yes?”

Of course this was the case. Both ovaries were affected and some fluid found contained cancer cells too. Because of that I was to see an oncologist and the possibility of chemotherapy was mentioned too. What flooded into my mind, and I don't believe that this was denial of disease, was, “Jesus is Lord” - the real knowledge of him being in control. I told this to the surgeon, letting him know that would still be looking forward to taking my trip around the world. I saw his face relax as he started to talk about the holiday and for me to make sure that I informed the oncologist about these plans so that treatment would not interfere with them.

When the doctors left me I thought about John receiving the news and felt a little sad so I decided to ring Pastor Steve and asked him to speak to John and pray with him, making sure that John was trusting in God for himself. Unexpectedly a few minutes later, John arrived on the ward as he was visiting the outpatients department with Neil, our eldest son. I informed him of the results and he took the news quite well. There had been a lot of people praying for him. John had actually woken up in the night (that in itself is a miracle) and had read a few scriptures which had comforted him, giving him strength and peace.

Pastor Steve visited me after he had prayed with John. He confirmed that John really was all right about the news. Peace was upon him and his trust was in God. My GP came onto the ward to visit me and to receive the results at first hand. This blessed me to know that she cared, and she mentioned at that time, that she believed that chemotherapy would be a help.

A nurse who had just been told of my situation came up and put her arms around me. I smiled at her and made this comment, "I don't know what the future holds, but I know who holds the future and I trust Him." I visited with a few special nurses who had cared for me on many occasions. I was encouraged as they talked about me really succeeding in going to see my sister in New Zealand. They said to remember to send them a postcard just to prove it. Individual care was expressed by these nurses and the domestic ladies. I felt quite privileged to have got to know so many in a real way and I looked forward to sending the postcards.

An appointment was arranged with the oncologist before I was actually discharged. I was to go to the Radiotherapy Outpatients Clinic. I was to be dressed ready for discharge and taken over in a wheelchair to keep the appointment.

Although my wounds were healing nicely, in general I was feeling weaker because of my lack of ability to eat sufficiently. Getting ready for the appointment and discharge was making me become very tired.

The oncologist informed me that I could not be cured from cancer but chemotherapy may help. I explained my faith in Jesus as Lord and that any treatment would be subject to my planned trip. I do not believe that he understood me at that point. He wanted me to postpone the trip until I had received six months treatment. I refused. I asked if the treatment could be postponed till after my trip as I knew the treatment itself would make me ill. He said that I could be so sick with cancer by then that nothing would help.

When it became apparent to him that I was going ahead with the trip he wanted me to have four treatments before I went away. He knew that he couldn't force me to do anything, so when I agreed to have one and see how it affected me, we shook hands. We both wanted me at my best possible health for the trip, which was now only four months away. I was told to be prepared for a hospital stay of at least five days at Newcastle, to be arranged within a couple of weeks.

I knew that God was preparing a way for me to accept this treatment, but now that it was inevitable, I was a little uneasy. I remembered back to the testimony of the mature lady at our church conference. I specifically remembered that she had chemotherapy and yet was remarkably well when she had continued with her travel plans. I seemed to be in a similar position and her story encouraged me. Yet I knew that I would have to pray about the side effects of the treatment, giving it over to The Lord, before I could settle.

As I was returned to the ward I met up with one of the junior doctors. I informed him of the need to go to Newcastle for treatment. He said, "It's not fair." Quickly I replied, "I have never been told that life was fair. Did anyone tell you that life was fair? We have to overcome." At that, he hugged me and moved on.

I was really tired and drained by this time but I had a couple of hours to wait before John could pick me up and take me home. A nice rest on my bed was needed, but being such a busy ward, I found that my bed had already been stripped and reallocated to another patient. Resting in the day room did not bring as much comfort and I was very glad when John arrived onto the ward to take me home.

The boys were excited to see me and I had a visitor that evening which, although I enjoyed, added to my feeling of exhaustion. A slight cough which I'd had in hospital got worse, and by the time I should have gone up to bed the cough was making me vomit. I decided to stay downstairs in an upright position on the settee. I could not sleep and became increasingly disturbed with the cough, wind and vomiting. Then, in an instant, I felt that I was not going to get my breath and a picture flashed across my mind as if something was trying to strangle me, and at the same time a feeling that my faith in Christ was being mocked. I cried out to the Lord, repeating, "Jesus is Lord, Jesus is Lord" and it was gone.

I could have put it down to my imagination owing to my tiredness, but the picture was of the enemy. I believe it was a spiritual attack following the blessing of feeling God so close to me in hospital. The attack wanted to rob me. It made me feel threatened and that I could not get through these serious problems with ease, or even my life. But I knew that the enemy is a liar, and although I felt unwell, my trust rested in the faithfulness of My Lord.

I was pleased when morning arrived and I received consecutive phone calls from Sue and Janet who had both been concerned for me in prayer in the night. They each gave me bible readings from the same Psalm. As I read the particular scriptures I felt that they were my own heart's cry to God which had been given to them, for them to understand how to pray for me.

> My earthly life cleaves to the dust; revive and stimulate me according to your word.
>
> My life dissolves and weeps itself away for heaviness; raise me up and strengthen me according to the promises of your word
>
> Consider my affliction and deliver me, for I do not forget your law.
>
> Plead my cause and redeem me, revive me and give me life according to your word.
>
> Psalm Ch 119 v 25, 28,

I thank God that I did not experience another spiritual attack in the same way. I felt at that particular period of time, that I had put my arms around my Lord and that I had lifted my legs off the ground and wrapped them around him to cling on to him. I did it in order to move only with him, as my whole life seemed to depend on it. All of my personal prayers surrounded this picture of myself, hoping to be strengthened a little physically before the inevitable chemotherapy demanded more out of my body.

I was able to celebrate Christmas with the family. It included taking part in the Carols by Candlelight Service at our church, always a favourite of mine, before the first scheduled treatment on 2nd January 1990. Prior to attending the Watch-night service at church on New Years Eve, a thought from Psalm 23 was going through my mind. the verse, "though I walk through the valley of the shadow of death I will fear no evil." Pat, a mature lady in our fellowship commented on this verse after someone else had mentioned the verse in the meeting. She had been praying for me, sensed that my trust was in God, and had asked him what card and encouragement to give me. God had replied by directing her to a card with a picture of a shepherd, and she wrote a very inspiring commentary on Psalm 23. I was deeply touched to see how God had used Pat very simply, and yet, in such a profound way. I took this precious word of encouragement into hospital with me.

Not only was it a blessing to me, but also to some of the people that I met there. It underlined again the truth of God's control and presence with me no matter what I may have to go through.

Out of natural concern that John and I would be wise in decisions to be made at this time, John's brother, Lenny, was trying to encourage me to have the six months treatment and to postpone the trip. I really appreciated his love and care, but

Lenny could not understand from our point of view, which was in faith and trust in Jesus. He was a little scared for me but I was more concerned to obey the prophetic word. I told him that basically, he would have to wait and see the promise fulfilled: "I will go on the trip, I will be well, and I will go in Jesus name."

I was able to say openly that it would be better for us as a couple to take the trip no matter how seriously ill I might be on my return, rather than postponing and possibly not achieving it. I reaffirmed that he must wait, watch and see what God would do. As I finished speaking to him a doubt rushed into my mind that I would hurt those who loved me by doing something that seemed irrational in their eyes. I quickly sent up an "arrow prayer" to God requesting that he would show Lenny his faithfulness. I picked up my bible and was prompted to stop at a certain page. My eyes went to 2 Peter Ch 1 v 19-21. These scriptures confirmed to me that Sue had indeed spoken to me prophetically, and that the message was proving to be a light shining in this dark time. It was there to keep me looking forward to all of these good things in store instead of dwelling upon sickness, death and chemotherapy. I thanked God for speaking to me from his living word yet again.

Charities often bless sick children by taking them out of their environment of sickness and treatment by arranging similar trips. I am a child of God, and he was sending me on my holiday in exactly the same way, and I was willing to take him at his word.

Chapter 16

> For me to live is Christ and to die is gain. But if I am to live on in the flesh, that will mean fruitful service for me.
>
> Philippians Ch 1 v 21-22

The children were still on school holiday on 2nd January 1990, so we all went up to Newcastle together to my admission to the General Hospital. On arrival, we were disappointed to find that the boys were not allowed onto the ward at anytime owing to the nature of the treatments being given. There was a day room, but this was used by smokers and was not a suitable place to sit and visit with the boys.

This concerned Daniel the most as he realised that we were asking him to be brave and not see me for a few days until I returned home. In the past he had loved to play with his Aunty Jean's dog at Hartlepool but even the promise of this could not change the miserable look on his face. As far as he was concerned, this hospital stay was one too many for his liking. John took the boys to Jean's house at Hartlepool and returned to the ward that evening with a very sad letter from Daniel. I was quite taken with his sadness, but there was nothing I could do about it except send my love to him in a return letter.

Tests were carried out for forty eight hours before I was given my first treatment. At first I had no idea how long it would take to administer the drugs or how they would affect me. As I watched other ladies I soon got a good idea. I prepared myself for the worst as I observed that it could take up to thirty six hours on a drip for the drugs to be administered with vomiting occurring no matter how many drugs were given to counteract it. As I observed and talked to other patients on the ward I felt great compassion. They expressed fear, anxiety, bitterness and many other emotions about their diagnosis of cancer, its treatment and the subsequent awareness of the possibility of death. I just knew how real my Lord was to me in taking me through this, and giving me more incentive to share this reality with anyone who would listen.

To my surprise my treatment only took few minutes to administer and initially I was not troubled with vomiting. I praised God for all those who had been concerned enough to pray about the side effects at that time. I was soon home to share all of the news with Janet and giving Daniel plenty of cuddles.

After a week I was very aware of how the treatment did affect me, and although these problems were not as bad as I had expected, I did not relish the thought of further treatment. The Professor that I met at Newcastle had confirmed that I could not now be cured, but he hoped that the treatment would increase my survival time. He also explained that the cancer found in the ovaries was the same as had been found in my stomach, so I was still being treated for stomach cancer.

Although I understood this, I was unsure about the hope in the chemotherapy helping, as I had read in a drugs book that stomach cancer was unlikely to respond to chemotherapy. As I was very definite about the negative effect that it had on my life, I wanted to be sure about the positive effect it could have. I decide to seek the Lord about it, and having done that, I talked over my thought with my GP. I felt encouraged to write to the Professor to express my concerns about treatment and the fact that "No cure" had not placed a death sentence upon me, but gave me even more reason to live a fruitful life in the service of my Lord Jesus. As my trust was in God, nothing that the Professor could say could change my positive outlook.

The Professor replied with a very open and honest letter. He understood my concern and expressed his hope in the treatment helping without giving a guarantee. He left it open for me to stop the treatment if I wished. He expressed his support in whatever decision I made. His honesty encouraged me to have at least another treatment before making any decision. My health problems did not interfere too much with the work in the fellowship of prayer support, counsel and pastoral care which I was very involved in. It just had to slow down a little at times.

Before I was due my second treatment, a Minister from Norway came to share his experiences with ministers in the town of street evangelism and caring for those in bondage to drugs, alcohol and prostitution. The timing of these seminars coincided with my growing desire to ask the elders to pray over me against spiritual forces before I actually went on my trip abroad. During one of the meetings, the Norwegian

Minister asked if there was anyone sick and needing prayer. I was encouraged in my own spirit that it was the right time for me to stand. Those around me also confirmed this. I basically informed him what the problem was and he called three other pastors and his wife to join him in prayer for me.

The essence of this was a stand against the work of the enemy. Not only was I pleased that so many Men of God were praying for me at one time, but that they were praying under the anointing of God, in power. I felt God's presence as I opened myself up to receive all that God had for me. Later whilst on my own, I asked The Lord for his direction on the chemotherapy in the light of that prayer.

I received peace to have only the second treatment before my trip, and then to wait upon him to confirm if it was necessary to continue treatment upon my return to England. I did not need to be admitted to the hospital for my second treatment. I just had to stay long enough for my blood to be checked and for the drugs to be administered. Daniel was pleasantly surprised that I did not need to stay in hospital this time. In general Daniel had become very easily upset, frightened of the dark and being rather nervous at school.

Following the experiences of my first treatment, I did not take as many anti emetic tablets as I should have done, and consequently I was quite sick. This concerned Daniel as he watched me and wanted to comfort me. He knew that it was the treatment that was affecting me at that time and I told him that I would be better soon. I was still feeling quite rough the following Sunday and would probably not have gone to church had it not been a special day in a way. Pastor and the Elders were going to publicly recognise and confirm the ministry of Pastoral Care in Pat and myself by the "Laying on of hands."

Pastor explained that the ministry had been going on for some time, but now more people would feel free to come and share as they desired.

I was very tired and nauseated by the time that the service was finished, so I was pleased when the boys were unexpectedly invited to a free showing of a Walt Disney film at the local cinema. This gave me time to rest. When they came home Daniel came charging in with sweets, balloons and full of exciting things to tell me about the afternoon. My response was very negative as I reminded him how unwell I was feeling. I knew that it was the wrong thing to say to him, but once said, I couldn't change it.

The next morning I was feeling a little better but Daniel wasn't. He complained of stomach ache and did not want to go to school. I left him in bed and saw the others off to school. John was not due at work till later that day, so I shared my concerns about Daniel and the need to expose the true reasons of him not being well. We decided to talk with Daniel and it was not long before he cried out, "I think you are going to die. If the cancer doesn't kill you the horrible treatment will."

Despite me thinking that this was the underlying problem, it hit me hard to hear it from his own lips. We persuaded him to go to school with the promise that we would take him and speak to both his teacher and headmaster on his behalf.

Once we had settled Daniel into school returned home and prayed about the whole situation. By the time Daniel came in from school I had received my answer and directions. I sat the three boys down and instructed Neil and Philip to explain to Daniel exactly how they had felt about me being sick in the past and how they now saw the situation. I was proud of the two of them. Neil made Daniel feel that he did not have to be ashamed of his feelings, as he had suffered in the same way when I was first diagnosed with cancer. He explained how he was frightened and his body felt ill all of the time, but as I had not died then there was nothing to make him believe that I would die now. Philip expressed that he just trusted all of the things that God was saying and that there was nothing for him to get bothered about even though he did not like to see me being unwell.

I then drew a picture of large cells and small cells, bad cells and good cells. I explained why the treatment can make me feel ill now but help in the future. After this we asked God to help Daniel to feel better. I also encouraged Daniel by giving him a little teaching on how God was really there with us when we feel sad. He works from the inside and that we have to let him fill our thoughts with his thoughts. There was an immediate response of joy upon Daniel. I really believe that God touched him. When he returned to school his teacher observed the difference in him. As she talked with me later she believed that I had been inspired to speak to him in such a helpful way. I could give all the glory to God as a real and lasting work was done that particular day.

Around this time, my brother Peter finally committed his life to Jesus and decided that he would be the support that my sister Christine needed with her family. This indeed was a double blessing and very much an answer to my personal prayer as I had continued to have concern for the welfare of Christine and her children.

His new found relationship with Jesus let Peter recognise that God actually spoke to him directly and gave him answers to his own concerns. Well, I know this to be true, but to hear this from my brother was just amazing. He told me that God had confirmed to him that Philip's eyes were really healed, and although he had hoped in the past that I would be all right, he now knew in God, that I was. My spirit confirmed that this really was God speaking to him on both issues. I rejoiced with him. It was good to have my brother share my faith. He is such a deep thinker, so once it was confirmed to him that the bible really is THE TRUTH, there was no holding him back from seeking to know more of this truth.

A short time after Peter's conversion a meeting was arranged at Dad's house to collect correspondence and thoughts from the whole family to pass on to Margaret. That day was very special to see Peter was overcoming his grief at the loss of his wife, Christine was well after having her children home with her for a few months, and Maureen was looking strong in helping Brian overcome his problems after his accident. It was very evident that God had brought us through a difficult time for our family as a whole. We decide to stand together in acknowledgement of this and to give thanks to God. It was a very moving experience for us all as was witnessed in a letter that Dad wrote to Margaret explaining this particular meeting and the effects that it had upon him.

JESUS IS LORD.

All things were ready for departure. Janet and Stephen (the Anglican Curate) had moved to their own church at Edgeware on the edge of London. We had visited them a couple of times, and now they were in an excellent position to look after our car while we were away. They were going to accompany us to the airport and pick us up on our return. It was good to see them again, although they weren't too sure about my appearance. We arrived just as the Morning Service was finishing, and

Janet thought that I looked like a punk. I was getting quite used to my own skinhead appearance due to the loss of hair from the treatment. We had lunch and then we were on our way, very grateful for the hospitality shown to us by Stephen and Janet. God was with us and we were all excited to be heading for the other side of the world.

Chapter 17

> If we live, we live to The Lord and if we die, we die to The Lord. So whether we live or die we belong to The Lord.
>
> Romans Ch 14 v 8

As we went through passport control, John handed in his passport with himself and the three boys included. I had already given mine to the same officer and he had held onto it. I had to smile to myself as he then asked John how many children he had, and then he did a head count. He asked which one was his wife. I was pleased to be mistaken for a young boy rather than being looked upon as a sick woman.

The twelve hour flight to Los Angeles was tolerated quite well by all of us and after an exciting drive from the airport to our hotel, we were soon settled down in our rooms for a good restful night sleep. Disneyland was the priority attraction the next day. This was within walking distance of our hotel, so as soon as breakfast was over we set off to spend the day there. Until that time I still had not felt very strong with my energy levels dropping quite quickly if I ventured out on a shopping trip in Darlington.

This particular morning I knew that God was being faithful to his promises as I felt well and full of energy. We walked around Disneyland for eight hours, enjoyed every moment of this and then walked back to our hotel. I had no ill effects. The rest of our time in Los Angeles was packed with more exciting things to do and see. At times it became quite hectic. I could give all the glory to God to be just one of many tourists and having sufficient energy to keep up with John and the boys as we enjoyed all of the sights.

Another flight of just over twelve hours from Los Angeles went well. We were all too excited to sleep even though we travelled all through the night. We arrived at Auckland Airport at 6am New Zealand time. Margaret and her family were there to meet us. They had got up at 2am to do so.

I'd had no recent contact with Margaret, so she had no idea of how well I would be or how much the journey would affect me. She had watched someone being brought out of the arrivals area in a wheelchair and expected it to be me. When I did appear, she took me to be Neil instead. She looked past me still waiting to see someone coming through who would match her expectations. When she realised it was me, full of energy and health she could only be amazed and give glory to God.

Obviously she observed the weight loss and the hairstyle looked different (close cropped hair was quite fashionable) but both Margaret and Peter were so pleased to see me looking quite well.

It took a couple of hours to drive to Margaret's home city of Rotorua. I made full use of the time by giving her the fuller details that I had left out of my letters. In general Margaret is a good listener and being a nurse herself, she was very interested in both the medical and spiritual matters. Peter does not share our faith and doesn't enjoy medical matters so I probably bored him. It was a good job he was driving. The children reacquainted themselves but soon started to show signs of tiredness. I was far too excited to feel tired. I later found out that Peter had commented to Margaret that once the adrenaline had stopped pumping in me they would see that I would probably need a lot of care.

Three weeks later Peter had to admit that he had been wrong, as apart from suffering a viral infection with a few other members of the family, I did not show any signs of serious illness. We spent four weeks and four days with Margaret and Peter and their children Ainsley, Lisa and Sarah. Margaret's house was twice if not three times as big as ours, so the ten of us fitted in quite well. We worshipped The Lord together at Margaret's church and were made to feel very welcome. I got involved in the ladies' bible study group and was encouraged to share my experiences and to pray with them. I also met with old acquaintances from my previous trips to New Zealand. They had followed my progress through Margaret and were pleased to see me looking so well.

Rotorua is situated in a particularly beautiful area with forests, lakes and mountains all around. It is a well known tourist centre attracting visitors from other countries to see the thermal activity in its famous geysers. The Maori culture is put across to the visitors in many entertaining and interesting ways and we have not tired of going to their concerts, seeing their meeting houses and craft work.

The pace of life is slower in New Zealand than in England with much less population and traffic. Anyone would enjoy a holiday in this part of the world. It was quite educational for the children but for me it was Margaret's company and praying with her that made the whole trip worthwhile. We remain very close as sisters even though many miles separate us. It was good to see how we had both grown in our faith and how specifically God was at work in each of us. As we parted, we both sensed that we would be seeing each other again in the not too distant future.

I had been quite proud of the boys' behaviour during our stay and wondered if they could keep it up as we spent the next eight days with Uncle Frank and his family.

Thankfully it was a shorter flight from Auckland to Melbourne as we moved on to another holiday. New Zealand had been like home, but none of us had been to Australia before. Uncle Frank was there to meet us at the airport, and as he was amazingly like my dad in looks and nature, even Daniel had no problem in recognising him. I had thought it better not to tell Uncle Frank and Aunty Rene about my recent illness in letters I had sent them. I thought that they would worry about me travelling and what care might be needed as I spent time with them. Now I could relate all of the details as Uncle Frank asked questions and could see for himself that I had recovered.

It was good to meet with cousins and their families that we had never met before. The hospitality was excellent and we were chauffeured to various tourist spots. One in particular is called

Philip Island where penguins come out of the sea at dusk and walk up the beach in groups to their burrows. This was a truly extraordinary sight and a highlight of our time in Australia. We were also introduced to Australian Rules Football. At first there didn't seem to be any rules, until we got used to it. All of Frank's family were involved either as a coach, players or supporters. The boys' behaviour did remain good and I was proud to hear people comment on it. The week was over too soon.

Having been away for a total of six weeks we were ready to go back home, but the journey ahead was rather daunting. To get from Australia to Heathrow meant two flights with just a couple of hours in transit at Singapore. The last flight was the longest of all at just over fourteen hours.

As we landed at Heathrow Airport there was a message awaiting us. Stephen and Janet had gone on holiday themselves but had arranged for a member of their church to meet us, take us to her house for refreshment, then to Janet's house to pick up our car, then send us on the last leg of our journey home. The lady had to get up at 4am to do this for us. We were very grateful and thanked God for her sacrifice.

It was good to be back with my church family. I had missed them the most whilst on holiday. As most of the congregation had prayed for us before leaving on our trip, they were all very interested to see how their prayers were answered. Some of my friends had written to me and I had valued their correspondence.

As I attended the hospital for a check up with the surgeon my mind was made up concerning chemotherapy treatment. I had felt God's confirmation about this whilst in New Zealand in two ways. Firstly, as Margaret worked as a nurse in the City Hospital she had taken me into the hospital library and I had looked at statistics for the treatment I was receiving. I know that statistics can prove or disprove almost anything and that they may have no bearing on me as an individual, but I was feeling very well and had no desire to become ill again just because of the treatment. Secondly I had shared my thoughts with the Pastor's wife at Margaret's church. She reminded me that John should have the last word on the subject, and that if John chose for me to carry on then I should do so. Of course I agreed with this for none of us live unto ourselves alone.

I talked with John and he allowed me to refuse more chemotherapy no matter what the consequences were. The surgeon was genuinely pleased to see that I had put on weight, my hair had grown and that my decision to stop the treatment was well founded. He did say that there were not many people who could do what I was doing, but that he was getting to know me much better. I did not know which way to take that comment at first but decided that it was probably a compliment.

The next visit to hospital was to see the oncologist. He supported me in my decision and agreed that we would work together in partnership about any future treatment that may be necessary. I asked a question about the "No Cure" prognosis. His reply basically inferred that even if I stayed well, the diagnosis of cancer remains, and that the effect of it upon my body could reoccur at any time.

I did understand his frankness and welcomed it in one way, but I wanted to have a good talk to the Lord about how I should understand this in Him. As I sat before the Lord in prayer thoughts rushed into my mind. I recognised that this was the

Spirit of God speaking to me. My trust was in Jesus, not in my health. My life was spared at this time because of his purposes and plans that He desires to fulfil in my life. There is no guarantee for me that cancer would or would not reoccur in the future. That is not for me to know.

BUT Jesus is Lord. His name is above the name of cancer. Cancer has no authority to take my life because it desires to. Jesus has ALL authority, and I am His. These thoughts prompted by The Holy Spirit brought peace. I did not have to think about cancer returning but to live this life today to the glory of The Lord.

Since the hysterectomy operation whenever people have asked if I am cured, I have never felt at peace to say yes, nor did I feel at peace to talk as if cancer was operating in my body now. It was easy to say that I was well and that I trusted the future to Jesus. I also found it was less important for me to think about long life than to think of a life of obedience to God. The verse of scripture in Romans 14:8 confirming that Jesus was in charge of life and death and that if God called me home now, I was ready. Paradoxically, the more I felt ready to be called home if God so desired, the more God revealed that I would be working for him for many more years to come. My view of God was constantly increasing, enabling me to trust and surrender all the more to him in the expression of obedience to God being better than life itself.

For a few months my health was quite good, but after suffering a chest infection, I was left with an irritating cough. After one particular coughing bout I felt an enlarged gland in my neck. I was curious as to the cause of this enlargement and wondered if it had anything to do with the cough. After ten days it was still enlarged, I was having a check up with the consultant surgeon and so I mentioned it to him. He sent me for a chest x-ray and arranged an appointment with the oncologist for the next day. Next day I was getting ready to keep the appointment. John was in bed after working a night shift. I did not want to disturb him so I sat at the top of the stairs to comb my hair. As I looked to the bottom of the stairs I was suddenly reminded of the time that I fell down the stairs.

At that time I believed that I could get no lower physically, mentally or emotionally and that the only way was up. The Lord told me to look where I was now – right at the top. I smiled to myself and thought this lump is probably not cancer this time.

At that point the telephone rang. It was Sue ringing to say that she had just been in prayer for me, and that she was sticking her neck out to say that the lump was definitely not cancerous this time. I told her of my own experience and that her words confirmed what God just spoken to me.

I knew that I could not speak to the oncologist as freely as I desired, but I was not ready to accept any treatment unless they confirmed why the gland was enlarged. Apparently the particular tumours that I had in the past had been rare and unpredictable, so the oncologist was just as curious as I was to see what we were dealing with this time. He did inform me that it would normally be quite routine to go ahead and treat with radium in other patients, but in my situation he agreed it would be wise to have the gland removed and examined.

I was soon admitted for a short stay in hospital to remove the gland but at discharge it would be seven days before biopsy results would be known. During that week I was interested to watch a television programme about cancer. At one point a list of cancers with their subsequent statistical survival times was on the screen. It seemed that every cancer was mentioned except stomach cancer. I was starting to think that it was because in general the prognosis for stomach cancer is poor. Then the commentator explained that the medical profession had not yet been able to improve the survival rate statistic of only 10% of all victims reaching five years survival from diagnosis.

All of the family were watching and Daniel asked me if I would be one of the 10%. I answered him quite simply by saying, “Yes God wants it that way.” What a look of joy there was on the oncologist's face as he read out the biopsy result. The gland had been enlarged but not malignant. I let the oncologist know that God had told me the result would be this. We laughed together as he informed me that the Professor at Newcastle had believed that it was definitely going to be malignant. He was now looking forward to tell the Professor that it wasn't. Later whilst talking to Margaret on the telephone in New Zealand about the result Daniel kept shouting “Tell her you are one of the 10%, tell her you are one of the 10%!”

I know that I am very privileged to walk this life with My Lord. I hope that more than 10% of the people will know this truth too.

Epilogue

> My grace is sufficient for you. For my power is made perfect in weakness.
> Therefore I will boast all the more gladly about my weaknesses so that Christ's power may rest on me.
>
> 2Corinthians 12:9

As I commenced to write this book in obedience to the promptings of the Holy Spirit, I was also preparing for a Celebration and Thanksgiving Service to God for my life to be held on the occasion of my 40th birthday. It was indeed a beautiful evening captured on videotape, forever to be remembered for God's grace and blessing upon all of the activities.

I had invited those who touched upon my life in many different ways. This included the family in the corner shop, the chemist and his wife, my hairdresser, my neighbours and many more who have shown their care and concern for me over the years.

My natural family were well represented as were my spiritual family. God put his seal upon the celebrations in a very particular way when Judi, who I had met previously in hospital, arrived to say that she had just come to know Jesus for herself. We had kept in contact and over months she had asked many searching questions about my faith. Apparently the Psalm that I had read to her in hospital had been brought back to her attention again, and God had revealed himself to her. I could not have asked God for a better birthday present.

I have continued to have ups and downs in my physical health. On the occasions that I have sought the Lord about this I have received the comfort that is in the scripture 2 Corinthians Ch 12 v 9. I have found it to be very real in my life as God has used difficult situations to his glory in a remarkable redeeming way. My peace remains as I surrender all unto him continuously, and he gives to me the way out.

I live with the diagnosis of cancer upon my life therefore if I have any symptoms the doctors need to eliminate cancer first. I can see that God even uses these situations to increase the trust and faith in God of those who surround me, especially John. I am pleased when tests prove negative because all of the glory goes to God.

I am not my own. I have been bought with a price. The price was paid for me at Calvary. I desire to know him who paid the price, His purposes and his plans. I know he will direct me. He hasn't failed me yet. Where he takes me now with him I have never been before. I trust him, for he is the way. I acknowledge my weakness and dependence upon him openly. I am very weak but he is strong in me. I do not desire to hinder him working in me in any way, as there is nowhere else to go, as he has the words of eternal life.

I know for sure that I am not immune from trouble. Things will try to come against me in the future but I rejoice "In the Shadow of his Wings"

Psalm 36 (AMPC).

1 O God, You are my God, earnestly will I seek You; my inner self thirsts for You, my flesh longs and is faint for You, in a dry and weary land where no water is.

2 So I have looked upon You in the sanctuary to see Your power and Your glory.

3 Because Your loving-kindness is better than life, my lips shall praise You.

4 So will I bless You while I live; I will lift up my hands in Your name.

5 My whole being shall be satisfied as with marrow and fatness; and my mouth shall praise You with joyful lips

6 When I remember You upon my bed and meditate on You in the night watches.

7 For You have been my help, and in the shadow of Your wings will I rejoice.

8 My whole being follows hard after You and clings closely to You; Your right hand upholds me.

9 But those who seek and demand my life to ruin and destroy it shall [themselves be destroyed and] go into the lower parts of the earth [into the underworld of the dead].

10 They shall be given over to the power of the sword; they shall be a prey for foxes and jackals.

11 But the king shall rejoice in God; everyone who swears by Him [that is, who binds himself by God's authority, acknowledging His supremacy, and devoting himself to His glory and service alone; every such one] shall glory, for the mouths of those who speak lies shall be stopped.

Post Script

Sadly for the family and all who knew her, Barbara had a recurrence of cancer and following surgery in December 1991 she passed way on 11th January 1992. Barbara left this Earth and The Shadow of his Wings to enter Heaven into the full light of the Presence of Her Lord, to see him and know him as he really is, and to receive her reward.

Barbara, Daniel and Philip in Disneyland

Barbara and Margaret

Mam, who's your friend

Barbara on the Hollywood Walk of Fame

40th Birthday Celebration